I0040623

MURRAY RAPHEL
REMEMBERS

MURRAY RAPHEL
REMEMBERS

BRIGANTINE MEDIA

Murray Raphel Remembers

Copyright © 2010 by Murray Raphel

All rights reserved. No part of this book may be reproduced or utilized in any way or by any means, electronic or mechanical, including photocopying, recording, or any information storage or retrieval system without permission in writing from the publisher.

Published by: Brigantine Media
211 North Avenue, Saint Johnsbury, Vermont 05819

Cover and Book Design by: Jacob L. Grant

Printed in Canada

ISBN 978-0-9826644-0-7

Other Brigantine Media books include:
It's About Time by Harold C. Lloyd
Am I the Leader I Need To Be? by Harold C. Lloyd
The Big Picture: Essential Business Lessons from the Movies
by Kevin Coupe and Michael Sansolo
Business Success in Tough Times by Neil Raphel, Janis Raye and Adrienne Raphel
Win the Customer, NOT the Argument by Don Gallegos
Selling Rules! by Murray Raphel
Crowning the Customer by Feargal Quinn

For more information on these books, please contact:
Brigantine Media
211 North Avenue, Saint Johnsbury, Vermont 05819
Phone: 802-751-8802
Email: neil@brigantinemedia.com
Website: www.brigantinemedia.com

Dedication

"The unexamined life is not worth living"
—*Socrates*

This book is dedicated to Ruth, my wife, pal, partner, greatest cheerleader and editor of this book.

I complimented her on the excellent editing and asked what was her secret? She replied, "When editing the book, I hear your voice."

Author's Note

This book has been a gratifying journey for me, reflecting on the joy of a full life, great family, and many, many good friends, associates, and clients.

I know there are people who were important in my life, but are not included in this book because our time together did not fit in with one of my stories. You are in my heart and memory.

Thank you, Neil and Janis, for publishing this memoir.

Contents

Chapter One

The Beginning

152nd Member Of Family

"**B**orn – a son, Murray Stanley Raphel, to Mr. and Mrs. Harry Raphel, 274 Tenth Street, Troy, New York."

This is a notice that greeted the public eye in Troy, New York, Sunday, January 28. But it did not tell the whole story.

From the Troy Record, shortly after my birth:

"To begin with, Murray is the 152nd latest member of perhaps one of the largest families in this part of the country and probably elsewhere. A family reunion shortly after his birth resembled a convention and heaped at his cradle was a ton of gifts that will carry a lasting memory of the big occasion for some years to come.

"A survey of the family reveals that Murray has two grandmothers, one grandfather, two great grandfathers, two great grandmothers, eleven great aunts, nine great uncles, a half dozen aunts and uncles and any number of cousins.

"This big family, all blood relations, are scattered throughout Troy, northern New York and Western Vermont. The oldest member of the four generations is Abraham Rosen, eighty-three, of Center Rutland, one of Murray's four great grandparents.

"Murray's mother, formerly Miss Sarah Rosen, is the daughter of Gussie Rosen of West Rutland. Mr. Raphel's parents are Abraham and Pauline Raphel of Troy.

"Mr. and Mrs. Abraham Rosen are the parents of Michael Rosen, the late husband of Mrs. Gussie Rosen who is the mother of Sarah Raphel, the mother of Murray.

"Mr. and Mrs. Raphel were married three years ago and Murray is their first-born. There were some three hundred guests at their wedding. The couple came to Troy shortly after their marriage and Mr. Raphel now conducts a grocery business at Tenth Street.

"They have great plans for Murray's future. As a matter of fact, they have set their minds on this point: No doctor or lawyer for him. Murray is destined to be a successful businessman, and in the words of his parents, 'Why shouldn't he be successful, even if he didn't do business with anyone but his relatives?'"

Wynantskill

Life began for me in Troy, New York with Sara and Harry Raphel, loving and devoted parents. I have early happy memories of car rides to my grandmother's house in Rutland, Vermont with the two senior Raphels belting out humorous songs in unison. Sometimes they left me there for the summer, as they worked several jobs during the Depression years.

That was not a problem. Gussie Doloff (my mom's mother) was a wonderful inspiration to me. She raised six children as a widow plus two more when she remarried, all of whom were devoted to her because of her very wise and kind manner. I was lucky to spend time with my grandmother.

My father was an insurance salesman for the Metropolitan Life Insurance Company. When he joined the company, the older agents had taken most of the best insurance routes. But if he was interested in working in the rural communities outside of Troy, New York, the largest city in the county, a route could be available for him in one of those areas.

Driving around, he found a small country town in the suburbs called Wynantskill. The name is Dutch because of the early exploration of the area by explorer Henry Hudson who was hired by the Dutch East India Company to look for a ship passage to the East from Amsterdam. He did discover a large river that he named the Hudson River after himself.

Later, one of the small country towns incorporated in its name the Dutch name "kill" for a small creek that ran through it coupled with the name of the person that first landed there. His last name was "Wynant" and thus, the community's name became "Wynantskill."

My mother enrolled me in the town's one-room school that held two grades in the same room. At Christmas, we put on a play and I had the role of King Wenceslas (from the song of the same name). I wore a crown cut out of cardboard and a glued-on beard. I stepped in front of the class and sang this song:

Good King Wenceslas looked out on the Feast of Stephen
When the snow lay round about, deep and crisp and even
Brightly shone the snow that night though the frost
*   was cru-el*
When a poor man came in sight gathering winter fu-el

(A song I sang 80 years ago.)

I finished the song and, to my amazement, the class stood up to give me a round of applause.

I still remember the excitement I felt at that moment, thinking, "So this is what show business is like!" and "Wow! I'd like to do this more often."

And, of course, I did a form of show business in future years with my speaking.

When I graduated from the Wynantskill's elementary school

ready for high school, the problem arose—what high school? I had two choices: to take a bus to Troy High every day where I'd be with my city fraternity friends or go to the high school in Averill Park whose students came from a dozen small rural communities including Wynantskill.

That was an easy decision for me: go to Troy High and be with my city friends.

My father disagreed. He felt Averill Park High was a better choice. Their school bus would pick me up every day right at my Wynantskill home and I'd have a new group of friends.

Despite my protestations, my father persevered, holding out the option, "If you're unhappy after your first year there, I promise you can transfer to Troy High."

I immediately started counting the days to the time when I could transfer to Troy. However, after a few weeks, I began to change my outlook. I began to feel the friendliness of my rural community by the way the students on the bus greeted me.

Since my father sold life insurance to many parents of the students on the bus and the students knew my father's name was "Harry," they took to calling out when I entered the bus, "Hi, Little Harry." It seemed a little odd since I was already a few inches taller than my dad. But if that name meant instant acceptance to the group, it was worth the "Little Harry" bit. My father thought it was funny and wondered if he came on the bus with me would they yell out, "Hi, Big Harry!" I quickly persuaded him not to test the waters and he reluctantly agreed.

Averill Park High school matriculated only a few hundred students, mostly girls at that time since many of the older boys were either drafted for World War II service or enlisted on their own. I did have some excellent teachers and made friends with people I would always remember.

One school day I will never forget. I came home from Averill Park High School to hear an outstanding piece of news from my mom. She was pregnant! A few months later my brother Arnold was born—fifteen years my junior. It was a strange feeling at first having a sibling after being an only child for so many years. Since I was so busy with my own high school life, I soon took the new arrival in stride.

Arnie went to the same small elementary school in Wynantskill that I attended; however, when it was time for high school, unlike me, he decided to go to Troy High. (Great! At least one of the Raphel boys made the switch.)

Arnie's future included becoming a Foreign Service officer for the State Department in Washington, DC and then the US Ambassador to Pakistan.

More about Arnie later...

Best Friend: Ted Simonson

Ted, a year ahead of me at Averill Park High School and my best friend, was an excellent writer and self taught gifted illustrator. We became each other's critic for our individual stories. One day we decided to write a play together based on high school life. We titled it "Adam Had It Easy." The plot line centered on the usual problems of high school student relationships. We received permission from a local fire station to use their building to stage the play there and had a great reception from local students and adults.

Ted and I continued to write stories, mailing them to one another for respective criticisms.

Baseball Friend: Elroy Face

I played right field on my high school's baseball team. I was a good fielder and average hitter. Amazingly, our small rural school made it into the state finals and won the New York State championship.

We played the championship game a few miles from nearby

Albany at the Hawkins Stadium, the home of the Boston Red Sox farm team.

I played right field and Elroy was our star pitcher. When anyone asked me if I were nervous playing the State championship game, I'd say, "Why would I be nervous? Elroy is pitching!" Few opposing batters ever got a hit off him. I remember he would greet an opposing team player laughing and saying, "You might as well go back to your dugout because you're not getting a hit from me today." And they rarely did.

After graduation Elroy was signed by a minor league team and eventually joined the Pittsburgh Pirates. He was an outstanding relief pitcher. His most productive season was in 1959 when he posted an 18-1 record with 17 victories in a row, earning the highest single season winning percentage in major league history. His 96 career relief wins ranks him fifth in the all-time list, tied with Walter Johnson for the most games pitched for one team (802).

(And that didn't include the games we played together at little Averill Park high school.)

Celebrity Friend: Jerry Lewis

The parents of comedian Jerry Lewis were a vaudeville team on the Borscht Belt circuit. Because of their traveling schedule, they left Jerry with relatives in Averill Park for part of his high school years.

We met in high school and did a few funny skits together in the high school auditorium. After high school I went to Syracuse University. Jerry launched his career on the entertainment circuit doing comedy acts such as humorously exaggerating the action of opera singers as their actual voices played on a record.

Jerry perfected his comedy act and landed jobs at the better nightclubs. He was booked into the 500 Cub in Atlantic City when he met Dean Martin and the famous comedy team was born.

When Ruth and I were married and living in Atlantic City, I read that Jerry and Dean were appearing at the 500 Club. I found out the name of the hotel where Jerry and Dean were staying. I went there to greet my Averill Park High School friend. When I spotted a bellhop who I knew from being a customer of our children's clothing store, I said, "I'm a friend of Jerry Lewis. Which room is he in?"

He took me to the room. When no one answered, he opened the door for me to wait for Jerry. When I entered the room I found it was true—Jerry was not there—but Dean Martin was sleeping on one of the twin beds.. He woke, looked up at me and asked, "Who are you and what are you doing here?" I answered, "I just wanted to say 'hello' to Jerry. We were a great comedy team before you came along." "Really?" said Dean and then, "Get out of here. NOW!"...which I quickly did.

And that was the one and only time I attempted to connect with my high school celebrity friend, Jerry Lewis.

I forgot all about this until I recently found my high school autograph book and this is what Jerry wrote:
"May your life be as Bright as Edison's first Electric Light."

In retrospect, I think his getting together with Dean was the right decision!

ABG Fraternity Friendships & 25th Anniversary

I still kept my friends in Troy by becoming a member and president in my senior year of a local fraternity, named ABG after the first three letters of the Greek alphabet: Alpha, Beta, and Gamma.

My presidency coincided with the 25th anniversary of ABG and we planned a big celebration. The important question for all the guys was what girl to invite to the festivities.

Milton Gordon was a member of ABG. After his discharge from the Army at the end of WW II, he went to Atlantic City with his friend Milton Kline for some "R&R." On the recommendation of a buddy, they stayed at Dichter's, a small family owned hotel in Atlantic City. It was there he met Shirley, the older daughter of the Dichters.

Would Shirley come to Troy as his date for the ABG dance? She agreed but needed permission from her mom. Mrs. Dichter (Jean) said yes, but only if Shirley's younger sister Ruth would also be invited (as chaperone). That seemed like an okay idea.

However, Milton had a difficult time finding a suitable younger fraternity member willing to take a chance on a blind date. When he asked me, a member of the younger set, if I would volunteer as the date, I hesitated. After all, I was the president of the fraternity and would be busy with many of the activities. Having to be responsible for an out-of-town date would take up too much time. But since I hadn't asked a girl yet, I told Milton to have Ruth send me her picture so I could see what she looked like.

The picture arrived a couple of weeks later. Ruth was very attractive. The photo had her posing on the front porch of her father's small hotel wearing a two-piece bathing suit. I decided to take my chances on Ruth!

A few weeks later I was at the railroad station with Milton when the train with the Dichter sisters entered into view. I stood on the platform looking in the train windows passing by. I suddenly spotted two girls looking at me. "Aha!" I said to Milton, "It must be Shirley and Ruth." I waved to them and made exaggerated funny faces as the train began slowing to a stop. They didn't respond.

So much for first impressions...

We welcomed them warmly and carried their bags to our waiting car. We drove to the home of Milton's cousin Elaine who agreed to have the two girls stay at her home. We helped them in with their luggage and said we'd see them later for the first night of the festivities,

During their stay, the four of us visited nearby Burden Lake where Milton's family rented a cottage for the summer season. I also took Ruth to Ted Simonson's home and introduced Ruth to Ted and his family.

Years later I asked Ruth when she first knew we would be a couple. She said, "The day you introduced me to Ted. I was impressed with him, liked his sense of humor and admired his taste in literature. I thought if he was your friend, then you must be OK. I agreed, which is why he was my best man at our wedding. Ruth and I spoke of Ted often. No wonder our son Neil's first word was "Ted."

Ted's personal commitment was to be a Methodist minister but he still continued to write. He became friendly with a motion picture director who hired Ted to write the screenplay for one of the first science fiction movies, "The Blob." This independent movie starred Steve McQueen in his first film. When the script was finished, Ted asked me to come to Downingtown, Pennsylvania, where the movie was being produced, for some input on the finished script. That was fun because we were back together again, writing.

Then Ted, having graduated college, enrolled in divinity school.

Back to Murray: After the ABG 25th Anniversary celebration and meeting Ruth, I started my matriculation at Syracuse University's School of Journalism.

Syracuse University

My father drove me to Syracuse to find a room in the city since all the college dormitories were filled. So many new students were attending college after World War II because of the GI Bill that gave veterans the benefit of a college education, housing and rooms nearby were at a premium.

We finally found a place near the University. The landlady said she would rent one of her apartments if three college students would agree to room together and pay her the monthly rent and utilities. Dad and I quickly found two incoming freshmen who seemed nice and were willing to share expenses.

My dad dropped off my clothes at the apartment. Since there were no hotel rooms available (with all the influx of relatives of the incoming and returning students) and without letting me know the problem, he bundled up in the front seat of the car to sleep that night.

The next morning we said goodbye to one another. Dad drove back home after saying, "So long, Little Harry. If you have any problems your mom and I are as near as your phone."

The next morning I went to the editorial offices of the *Daily Orange*, the daily campus newspaper put together by students every day, to see Paul Keil, the editor. I introduced myself and asked if I could work there as an intern. Paul looked at me and asked what experience I had. I told him I was the editor of my high school newspaper. Paul answered, "If you want to hang around for the next hour or so you'll meet about forty or more applicants also asking for a job and guess what: they all were editors of their high school paper."

I thanked Paul for meeting, but before I made my exit, I asked Paul where I could see copies of the *Daily Orange* from past years. He showed me the paper's library and I sat down to review pages dating back fifty years or more.

I went through a lot of humorous or just plain interesting anecdotes. By reading past issues and figuring out what the present *Daily Orange* lacked, I found a possible break through. I created a proposed column titled "Tradition Talk." With several columns written, I returned to editor Keil's office the next day with my three sample columns and asked his opinion. He said, "I've been looking for a humorous column to run weekly on the editorial page. We'll start with these."

Overnight I became a journalist!

News from home:

My father was involved in an auto accident. Because of a head injury, he developed some blackout moments; not enough for any major impairment but enough to keep him from driving on a regular basis. His injury precluded him from traveling his regular route to take care of his insurance customers.

Dad received compensation from Met Life and my mother jumped in with a solution for additional income. She was an excellent cook and with my father's help in creating a catering kitchen in the garage, she quickly established herself as a kosher caterer for families in the greater Troy area as well as communities in nearby Massachusetts. Her prices were reasonable and her food excellent, so she did well. My father joined her in business as the maitre d', greeting the guests as they arrived and escorting them to their assigned tables. Tall and good looking in his tuxedo and with his affable personality, he made every special occasion special.

Meanwhile, back at Syracuse I took enough courses to eventually graduate with two degrees—one in journalism and the other in drama.

I enjoyed my classes but constantly struggled with money so I decided to look for a part time job. I contacted the local shoe stores since I worked on Saturdays during my last two years of high school years selling shoes.

The Red Cross shoe store in downtown Syracuse was looking for part time help and they hired me to work Saturdays and Wednesday nights when all the stores were open. My weekly pay for these hours was $21. Aha! Just enough for a weekly food coupon booklet for $21, which enabled me to have 21 meals each week in the college cafeteria (three meals a day times seven days). This did mean missing the weekly football games. But the choice between football games and 21 meals was an easy decision.

At the *Daily Orange*, I was promoted to Director of the Editorial Page. I found some talented fellow students to write weekly columns. One writer was Melvin Elfin, who eventually worked for *Newsweek* magazine where he condensed his name to "Melfin." Another journalist undergrad was Jack Lavin, who authored a regular humor column on everyday happenings within the student body.

Jack and I teamed up to write some of the scripts for an original campus musical review, "Long Live Love." There was a talented comedian who wrote his own copy for the show, and Jack and I contributed additional material for his act. The comedian's name: Jerry Stiller.

Jerry Stiller, along with his talented wife and partner, Anne Meara, went on to fame with shows on radio, the stage, and TV. They received rave reviews for a series of radio commercials they created for Blue Nun wine. Together they gave several great performances on the Ed Sullivan weekly television variety show. Jerry received his best critical acclaim for his performance as Frank Costanza on the "Seinfeld" show.

Jerry also wrote a successful biography, "Married to Laughter." He kindly included a personal comment in the copy he sent me: "Murray, you are a part of my life! Love, Jerry Stiller."

Jack Lavin and Jerry Stiller are part of great memories from Syracuse days!

Stopover in Addison, NY, Wedding Plans & Troy, NY

After graduation from Syracuse, with my cherished journalism degree in hand, I sought a newspaper job. After sending resumes to many daily and weekly newspapers, I finally received one reply from the owner of the *Addison Advertiser*, a small weekly paper in upstate New York. The owner, Mr. Miller, said he'd like to have me come and talk with him.

I did and he hired me. I soon found out I was responsible for writing all the stories, taking all the pictures, and developing them. Essentially doing everything except work the linotype machine—all this for a salary of $35 a week.

It soon occurred to me to ask for a raise. I said to Mr. Miller, "I'm unhappy." He asked me, "What would make you happy?" I answered, "A five dollar a week increase in salary." He looked at me and said, "Well, I'm sorry to see you go."

My decision to leave was confirmed late that night by the unexpected appearance of one of my college roommates, Art Gruber. Gruber was a character similar to Kramer on the "Seinfeld" TV sitcom.

This is typical Art Gruber: We met one day for lunch at a restaurant in Syracuse. He informed me, "I've never seen Niagara Falls. I'm going tomorrow. Come with me." Since it was nearly a three-hour drive from school to the falls (and I had homework to do), I declined. A few days later I received a giant postcard from the Gruber. On one front was a big picture of Niagara Falls. On the back was this message, "Going over the falls in a barrel today at 3 pm. Pray for me."

And so it was in keeping with Art's persona that he awoke me out of a sound sleep in my Addison apartment by loud knocking on the front door accompanied by a high pitched shout, "Wake up! Wake up! The British are coming! It's time to leave!"

I opened the door and the Gruber looked at me and said, "What the hell are you doing in here? The whole town closes down at 4 pm in the afternoon. You don't belong here. It' s time for you to leave. There's an all night diner a few miles down the road. Let's go there and we'll talk." We did and he reinforced my decision to leave.

After Addison, I left for New York City hoping to find a better paying newspaper job. But I didn't have the experience the large publications demanded. Not sure what to do, I went to the main office of the Miles Shoe Company (located in New York) since I worked for Miles in Troy on weekends and vacation when I was in high school.

I was directed to the office of the personnel manager who

turned out to be Charlie Sparaco. Charlie was the manager of the Miles store in Troy when I worked there. Charlie was glad to see me and asked what I was doing in New York. "Looking for a job," I replied. "Great!" he said, "I've got an Assistant Manager's spot open for you in White Plains. It's a short train ride from New York. Get there before the store opens tomorrow morning. I'll call the manager to tell him you'll be there. The job is yours."

I thanked him and took the early train to White Plains the next morning arriving there about 8:30. The store wasn't open yet but there was a young man waiting in the vestibule. "You work here?" I asked him. "Yes." He said. "I'm waiting for the manager to open up. He has the keys."

As we chatted, he informed that he was newly engaged and happy to be working at a good paying job, looking forward to a promotion as the new assistant manager. "That's nice," I said. Suddenly I realized that no one had told him somebody else was getting the job—me! The manager then appeared and said to me, "Who are you?" I told him Mr. Sparaco sent me here for the assistant manager's job at his store. He looked at me and said, "Oh yeah, Charlie told me you'd be here." And then turned to his young salesman standing there, "Meet your new boss. Sorry."

That's how chain stores operated back then. I felt sorry for the young salesman but was distracted knowing I would be leaving that evening for a long weekend in Atlantic City to see Ruth. Despite the fact that I disliked the driving, I found myself visiting her every weekend.

After a summer of long distance romancing, Ruth and I both knew we were in a serious relationship. So, at the end of the summer, when I was back home in Wynantskill, I called my step grandfather, Morris Doloff, who was married to my grandmother Gussie and asked him for advice on an engagement ring for Ruth. Morris owned and operated a clock shop. His tiny store in Rutland, Vermont was like walking into Geppetto's workshop in "Pinocchio"—dozens of clocks ticking along with grandfather clocks announcing every hour. Knowing Morris had contacts with jewelers in New York, I asked him to buy a ring.

A few days later, my Uncle Irving was driving from his home in New York to visit Gussie in Rutland, when he stopped at our house and placed the ring (Morris had ordered for me) in our mailbox. He called my parents to have them tell me "the ring" had arrived!

On my next trip to Atlantic City, I made it official and gave Ruth the engagement ring. She was very pleased and later told me that she kept looking at the ring that night instead of sleeping.

Ruth and I started to make plans for our wedding in November. Since I was now working as an assistant manager of a Miles Shoe Store in Albany, we decided to look for an apartment in nearby Troy. We found an unusual and delightful apartment in a brownstone that was originally built by the designer of he Monitor Submarine in the Civil War. It had 15-foot ceilings and a staircase in the living room that led to our alcove bedroom overlooking the living room. In the meantime, I was promoted to manager of the Albany store.

When we moved in after the wedding and our Miami honeymoon, Ruth found a secretarial job in the office of a successful Albany attorney, just a few blocks from the shoe store I managed. We drove together to work every morning, met for lunch most afternoons, and then rode home in the evening to our apartment.

A few months later when she found out she was pregnant and the apartment situation looked bleak, she suggested we move back to Atlantic City to be close to her family and look for a business opportunity. I said, "Let's go!"

Chapter Two

The Atlantic City/
Gordon's Alley Story

Atlantic City, Here I Come!

We arrived. Ruth's mother and father gave us a room in his hotel until we found our own apartment.

I planned on going to local shoe stores in Atlantic City for a job and Ruth would ask around for secretarial work.

When we told my father-in-law, he said, "Why don't you both work with Milton and Shirley in their retail children's shop? You could be partners!"

The partnership began. Our contribution to the partnership was our Chevy automobile that had taken us to Florida and back for our honeymoon and our wedding gift money loaned previously to the Gordons to help Shirley pay some of her suppliers' bills.

When I called my father about this small investment on our part to be partners in an established business, he thought about it for a moment and then said, "But remember, they're getting you." (Nice words from a father to his son!)

After signing the papers, we went to the store we now shared with Shirley and Milton. They showed us the inventory and their apartment in back of the store. It had a bedroom, bathroom, kitchen and living room. Shirley suggested we move in with them and sleep in the pullout bed in the living room. We accepted the offer.

Since money was tight, Shirley, who was pregnant with her second child, could share her meager maternity wardrobe with Ruth by switching dresses back and forth.

After a few weeks, Ruth's dad asked me how things were going.

I said the four of us got along all right but there wasn't enough business to draw a decent salary. He had a story and a suggestion: "When I lived on New York City's East Side, there was a man who owned a men's clothing store. He went house to house to collect a $1 a week. After twenty weeks he had $20 of the customer's money, enough for them to buy a suit in his store. Why don't you do the same thing?" he asked.

And so we did.

Milton and I split the addresses of people living in Atlantic City and the suburbs. We knocked on doors of all the homes and when the woman in the house answered we gave this memorized speech:

"Good morning (or afternoon). My name is Murray Raphel (or Milton Gordon) and we have Gordon's Children's Shop in Atlantic City. We are starting a club that will save you money for your children's clothes. Here's how it works. I come to your house every week to collect a dollar for your club. At the end of ten weeks we will give you eleven dollars for the ten dollars you have saved in your club to spend on clothes in our store. In addition, we will have a drawing every week and one of our club members will win a fully paid up card!"

We knocked on several hundred doors and succeeded in signing up 300 members. This meant we had increased our customer base by 300 new families for the club's ten weeks. That enabled us to take a little extra money for our weekly salaries.

Our growing business faced a new problem. Atlantic City's first large discount store called Garwood Mills opened in an old trolley barn in the inlet. In their infant and children's department, many of the brands of clothing were the same as we carried, but they sold them at much lower prices.

We needed to change our direction quickly. At about the same time a larger building became available for sale just a few blocks from our present location. Between our two families we had just enough money for a down payment by selling our new homes in the suburbs. We still needed to secure a mortgage from the bank.

The new three-story building was much larger than our present store. The first floor space was not only ideal for our store but we had room to expand our size range.

There were apartments on the remaining two floors. The Gordons decided on the third floor and we took the second. Besides, there was a small rental apartment available on both floors. The arrangement sounded good to all of us.

And then we were faced with a new decision. The most prominent children's store in town, Spears, had a major fire and offered sell us their undamaged merchandise below their wholesale cost. They offered to lease us their property at a reasonable rent and, as an added benefit, we could use their name.

My father-in-law and his wife (Herman and Jean Dichter) were on vacation in Florida. He called to see if the bank had given us the mortgage for the new building. I said, "Not yet, but it seemed okay." I also told him of the new opportunity to take over the Spears store instead. This was his reaction, "Don't do anything until I get back. Jean and I will leave Miami in the morning and drive straight through to Atlantic City. We'll talk about it then." When he arrived he came directly to our small store, walked up to Shirley and asked her, "What's your store's name?" She answered, "Gordon's." He said, "That's right. Don't ever use somebody else's name." We all agreed. The mortgage came through. And we started putting plans together for the new larger store with the name "GORDON'S" in big letters on the front of the building.

Beginning of Writing and Traveling

I continued writing in the evening while putting most of my daily effort into growing Gordon's business. Mostly I wrote short fiction stories and magazine articles. They were quickly returned with rejection letters. Ruth insisted I keep at it. In exasperation and frustration, I finally said to her, "If you think it's so easy, why don't you write something yourself and send it to a publisher?" And so she did.

We had a difficult time finding toys for son Neil to play with because of our limited budget. Ruth solved that problem by collecting different sizes of cardboard boxes and added kitchen utensils, placing them on the floor in our living room. This gave our baby Neil safe and creative ways to play.

Thinking other parents might have a similar problem, she wrote a story on the problem and her solution. She titled it, "Playtime for Baby," and sent it to *My Baby* magazine. A few weeks later they sent her a check for $25. She said to me, "Didn't seem difficult for me." I promptly replied, "Beginner's luck."

We had just moved into a new home in the suburbs. Neil missed his old friends and couldn't find new ones. Ruth saw this as a new problem needing a new solution. She decided to sit outside with him on the front steps of our house for several days with lots of treats in easy to reach containers. Before long, there were several preschoolers eager to meet the new kid on the block—another problem, another solution; another magazine article. She titled this story, "New Boy in the Neighborhood" and received another $25 check.

When I grumbled, Ruth reminded me, "Your stories are not about what you know. They are fiction. You should write about something you know and care about." What did I know about? The answer was retailing and the conflicts of running a small business.

Around the same time, a Philadelphia television station

announced a contest for an original play with the winner receiving a check $1,000 and a production of the play on the station. One of the judges was the well-known screenwriter and producer Dore Schary.

I wrote a play called "My Son's Business," entered it in the competition and WON! "Great!" I said to Ruth, "Now we can buy some new kitchen appliances and a sofa for the living room." (We had recently sold our home in the suburbs and moved into an apartment over our new, big store. We took the apartment on the second floor, directly over the store, and the Gordons moved into the same size apartment on the third floor right above us.)

Ruth stopped my practical suggestion for using the $1,000, saying, "No. We should go with the three children to Europe! How about a trip to Dublin, London, and Paris? Who knows when we'll get to Europe again?" (Of course she had no fortune teller's magic globe ball to see that in a few years she and I would be traveling more than 100,000 miles a year for more than ten years doing marketing seminars around the world.)

But for the present travel, destinations would be Dublin, London, and Paris.

Dublin

In Dublin, we stayed at the legendary Shelbourne Hotel, built in 1824, and the preferred place to stay for many celebrities through the years. The hotel faces Saint Stephen's Green, a beautiful landscaped park. We were just a short distance from famed Trinity College and Grafton Street, a pedestrian walk full of shops and restaurants (which gave me ideas for the future development of Gordon's Alley).

For sightseeing, we hired a very genial tourist guide, with a car, who took the five of us—Neil, Paula, Caren, Ruth, and me to well known places including Blarney Castle where, as historical legend has it, anyone who kisses the Blarney Stone will have a magic ability to speak eloquently. Perfect for my business.

Our guide pointed out the sights as we travelcd. I saw a roofer fixing a damaged thatched roof. I yelled out to him, "That's an old profession." He replied, "Well, I'm an old man."

As we drove the narrow, winding roads through the beautiful sights of green land and sea of the Ring of Kerry, our driver turned to Caren, our youngest, and said, "Keep your eyes open. You may see leprechauns along the way. Don't worry. They won't bother us. Look for the end of a rainbow because that's where they stand, guarding a pot of gold." Caren watched for a rainbow. Although none appeared, she was entranced the rest of the day by the possibility of meeting up with little men in green suits.

Throughout our Ireland travels we were captivated by the warmth and friendship of the Irish people then and whenever we returned for several future looked-forward-to business trips.

London

We had reserved an apartment in London before we made this trip. When we arrived, the owner of the apartment house met with Ruth and (ready for this?) took an inventory of all the cups, saucers, forks, knives, and spoons to make sure when we left there was the same amount as when we arrived.

She was also disgruntled when, after showing Ruth all the paraphernalia for making tea, Ruth asked, "Where are the tea bags?"

London was exciting for all of us and we visited the usual tourist sites—Windsor Castle, the Tower of London, the Changing of the Guard at Buckingham Palace and Westminster Abbey, where Ruth spent extra time at the "Poet's Corner," the burial spot for famous British authors. We also visited as many museums as we could without the children getting bored. Their favorite visit was to Barnaby Street, which was then the height of British fashion.

Right across the street from our apartment was a theatre

where we all went to see a production of Chekhov's "Three Sisters." It was a great evening's entertainment.

Through the years London has always been a favorite place especially for Ruth and me to revisit. I tell everyone I could drop Ruth somewhere in London and return three weeks later to pick her up and she'd ask, "How come you came back so soon?"

Now we were ready for the last city on our itinerary to visit...

Paris

Again, we visited the well-known places like the Louvre with its magnificent art collections, including the famed Mona Lisa, the broad boulevards such as the Champs-Élysées, walks along the Seine with the great architecture of Notre Dame Cathedral, and Montmartre.

On our last day before leaving for home, Ruth and I decided we would take the children to the Eiffel Tower and ride the elevator to the top for a great view of beautiful Paris, which we would all enjoy and remember.

As we were getting dressed to go, Ruth said to me, "Caren's complaining about not feeling well. I think she's coming down with a cold. You can take Neil and Paula to the Eiffel Tower and I'll stay in the hotel with Caren."

I was about to leave with Neil and Paula when suddenly I heard from Caren, "NO!" She had jumped out of bed and yelled, "I'm all better! I want to see the Eiffel Tower too."

And we all did!

Gordon's Alley

Once we established ourselves in the new large store, we began an all out effort for an upscale image. We looked for exclusive brands but with an inclusive attitude. We knew all economic classes of people liked buying nice clothes in a nice atmosphere served by nice sales people.

Gordon's became known for our European imports even though it was only about 10 percent of our merchandise mix. We made sure we also had popular-priced merchandise and national brands.

To enhance our business, we decided to create Gordon's Alley as the first inner city pedestrian mall in New Jersey, taking advantage of a new state law authorizing pedestrian malls in cities. Our goal was to create a premier shopping area in Atlantic City by offering quality merchandise and superior service. Our philosophy from the beginning was: "Find out what the customers want and give it to them."

Right next door to our new building was a narrow street called Presbyterian Avenue in recognition of the Presbyterian Church at the end of the street. We had the fortune of having the minister of the church agree to change the name to Gordon's Alley. There were seven small houses in this alley and the owner agreed to sell them to us at a reasonable price. We gave the owner a small deposit and agreed to pay the balance three months later.

In order to attract more customers with a diversified shopping experience, we then advertised for entrepreneurs to open retail shops in these houses. We sold each house for the amount of our purchase price. Between the Alley houses and stores in a building we purchased across the Alley on Atlantic Avenue, we had a leather shop, flower shop, toy store, men's boot shop, women's lingerie shop, and a high fashion women's Capezio shoe and clothing shop which we owned.

We also made the very necessary purchase of two empty lots facing South Pennsylvania Avenue and extending to Gordon's Alley for customer parking. But the prize retail establishment was a cheese shop in the Alley on the ground floor with a French style restaurant on the second floor looking out over the Alley. We knew customers wanted to shop in an attractive environment so we asked our good friend and brilliant architect Martin Blumberg to create Gordon's Alley's environment. When a reporter from the *Atlantic City Press* interviewed Marty on his design, this was his answer: "We tried to recreate the character that would exist in an early English village. We didn't have a long street to work with but we achieved the effect with subtle anglings of the buildings. We used three different types of paving materials that served as pathways leading to the stores."

Marty became so involved that the Gordons and Raphels jointly purchased with him a small run-down apartment building in the Alley and, with his design, turned it into smart looking offices purchased by a prominent out-of-town law firm.

Our next joint venture to complete the Alley was the purchase of a larger building in the Alley, a former garage for the Boardwalk National Bank. Marty wisely created a courtyard between that building, The Garage in Gordon's Alley, and Gordon's. Because of the free parking, the back door of our main store became the more important entranceway.

Besides Marty's office, The Garage also housed a stationery store and a brand new bookstore, opened by Neil Raphel and partner Cathy Linsk with a blockbluster appearance by famed author James Michener.

The Garage was large enough to house an artist who specialized in huge canvases and a small art movie theater on the top level of the three-story Garage.

When all the retailing was in place, we decided to have a huge opening promotion with radio stations present, a full-page ad in the *Atlantic City Press*, and, of course, a direct mail invitation to all our customers.

Gordon's Alley officially opened on Monday, August 13, 1973. Several thousand people came to celebrate opening day festivities with us. The newspaper interviewed customers and dignitaries.

Here are some of their quotes: "It's fabulous." "It's nice and innovative." "One stop shopping for the whole family." "What can I say? It's beautiful." "It's the beginning of the remaking of Atlantic City."

Politicians sent congratulations. Telegrams arrived

throughout opening day from the governor, the mayor, our congressman, county freeholders, state assemblymen and U.S. senators.

"If It's Saturday, It Must Be Gordon's Alley"

Retailers have always known that Saturday is the best shopping day of the week. Children are home from school. Adults working a 40-hour week have Saturdays to shop. Why not encourage them to come to Gordon's Alley?

Soon after we opened the Alley, we came up with this descriptive slogan that we used in our opening ad and continued using on every Saturday ad: "If it's Saturday, it must be Gordon's Alley." The phrase became a favorite with staff and customers.

A fun aside: Nick Scutti called to congratulate us that Gordon's Alley was the only official "Alley" in Atlantic City. In contrast there were many recognized streets, avenues, terraces and drives. He should know. Nick lettered most of the names on all these places.

We put our marketing skills to work in making Saturday special at Gordon's. If you arrived by walking in our front entrance, the windows grabbed your interest with a fashion story and a staff person greeted you. If you came by car and parked on our big lot on South Pennsvlania Avenue right next to the firehouse, you walked up the Alley to a pedestrian mall and you were a few steps away from the entrance to Gordon's and the many specialty shops along the way.

If it was lunchtime, you could stop at the Alley Deli and have a great lunch in the atmosphere of an old fashioned deli or relax at the Top of the Shop restaurant to enjoy a salad, sandwich or delicious dessert.

We made sure all the shops in our main store—infants, toddlers, girls, teens, men's and women's—featured designer clothing, many brands exclusive with us, but we also made sure there were always good buys for the bargain hunters. After all—if it's Saturday must be Gordon's Alley—had to be the best shopping for all our customers.

We tried to have a special "happening" every Saturday. One day a woman came to us with delicious homemade pies. Could she sell them in Gordon's Alley on Saturdays? The answer was "Yes." We called her "The Pie Lady" and advertised she would be in the Alley with her fresh delicious pies ONLY on SATURDAY. She sold out before noon!

An American Indian came to see us with samples of authentic Indian handicrafts. Could he sell them in the Alley on Saturdays? "Yes," we said; the same with the Italian baker and his cannolis; the same with various artists who filled the courtyard with colorful paintings and ceramics.

The customers loved our special Saturday sales. Women lined up for our offer of free makeup consultation at the Ralph Lauren cosmetic counter. The teens bought our Gordon's Alley tote bags in every color as an alternative school bag. On Saturdays, we had our monogramming lady Molly available for personalizing their bags.

At Christmastime we brought choirs from local churches to perform holiday songs on Saturdays and we served customers hot drinks and pastry inside the main store. Top of the Shop restaurant had Saturday breakfasts with Santa during the month of December.

The secret to success was piling one promotion on top of another to create excitement. An edict we always followed: if you could start a customer buying one item that was special, you could keep her shopping and shopping. We always had those special items on Saturday.

We realized the importance of our Saturday Alley concept when a local plumbing and heating company asked me to create a slogan like "If it's Saturday it must be Gordon's Alley" for their business. We politely declined. After all, that idea was already taken...

It's the Merchandise

For the Gordons and Raphels, it was "never the economy." It was always "the merchandise."

We would go to any legitimate extreme to find lines and suppliers that were not to be found in our competition. The style had to be right and the quality there. That meant going to all the New York trade shows, visiting the showrooms along Fifth, Sixth, and Seventh Avenues between 41st and 29th Streets or some buildings in the 50s to line up exclusivity promises with established lines we were after or look out for new lines we could claim for our very own.

That meant following leads to less known areas in dilapidated buildings or former hotels, up rickety staircases where new designers were holding court. We were always looking for the next great style.

Every season we made a pilgrimage to the fourth floor of Bloomingdale's New York 59th store. There is where they placed their newest trends and designers. Besides, we took note of their displays and signage. Their stylists were great teachers.

One of our best resources was our good friend Ab Rosenberg. We first met Ab when we opened a Capezio shop along Atlantic Avenue as we expanded from Gordon's to Gordon's Alley. At that time Ab was President of the Capezio's Children's Division. Later he left the company to open a Capezio shop in Greenwich Village. His staff consisted of mostly aspiring actors, actresses and musicians. The store was filled with avant-garde clothing. We made a pilgrimage there several times a year as Ab was very generous in giving us leads on his best sellers such as 52 Bond women's clothing and Kork-Ease shoes. But most importantly he gave us a quality, inexpensive producer of canvas tote bags.

We had the canvas tote bags silk screened with the Gordon's Alley logo and it became our biggest seller. We stocked them in every color available. It was the *de rigueur* school bag for every high school kid in Atlantic County and shopping bag for their moms. They were like miniature billboards, advertising our retail shopping center all over Absecon Island.

Then came another winning idea for the bags— monogramming. A great monogrammer in our area, Mollie Dobbins, joined the Gordon's Alley family. Mollie personalized the tote bags, but she was so fast and good, she was asked to monogram shirts, sweaters, knit hats, etc. and brought us lots of extra business and new customers, especially at giving time like Christmas.

In the early years of Gordon's Alley, the U.S. State Department sponsored a trip for European manufacturers to visit selected children's clothing retailers around the country. To our surprise and delight, Gordon's was chosen as one of the retailers. We found new and wonderful suppliers from France, Austria, and Italy. One of the lines, Absorba from France, became an established brand among higher-end children's stores. Because of the visit to our store, we were one of their very first U.S. importers. Shirley, who bought most of the infants' and children's clothing, made some of these brands the exciting centerpiece for her departments, especially the infants'.

Two other manufacturers became suppliers and friends: the Blums from Belfort, France and the Haideggers from Innsbruck, Austria. In fact, before Georges Blum returned to Belfort, we had our son Neil, who was a student at Swarthmore College, meet him at the Philadelphia airport, where it was arranged that Neil would work in his factory the following summer. And he did. We returned the favor and had the Blum's son, Patrick, work the next summer at Gordon's.

The Haidegger experience was a little different. Soon after meeting the Europeans and buying their merchandise, we decided to plan a trip to Europe with the help of our brother-in-law David Dichter, who was working and living with his wife Ruth and children, Alexandra and Ollie, in Geneva, Switzerland. We went to Geneva, Paris, Florence, and Innsbruck. It was our first and most memorable European trip. Most of the inner continent travel was by train where we had our first sight of the majestic Alps. I can never forget Ruth and Shirley screeching in the hallway of the train at their first sight of the mountains.

We spent a delightful two days in Innsbruck, Austria (which is completely surrounded by the Alps). Karl and his wife Ingrid entertained us at dinner in their home. The next day we visited their retail store and then looked at their coat line for export. Before we left, we made arrangements to have their daughter Nathalie spend a summer with us. She became one of the four European young people who came to Atlantic City and stayed in the home of the Raphels and Gordons.

Another good merchandise decision of ours was to identify Gordon's with Ralph Lauren. We started with the men's store, carrying every color in their short sleeve basic knit polo shirt. We gradually expanded our commitment to the men's line and added children's clothing when it became available. Then we added a separate department for the women's RL line, including shoes and handbags, and finally a prime area in our center store for RL cosmetics. Our relationship was such that the company sold to no other retailer in South Jersey until Macy's opened on the mainland...but we still maintained exclusivity among non-department stores.

But what really distinguished us and gave us customer calls from all over the country was a Finnish ski wear line by the name of Luhta. Ruth and I began visiting Helsinki, Finland for speaking engagements on direct marketing soon after I appeared at Montreux Symposium. On one such visit we saw advertising on the Finnish Fashion Fair held there every January. We took a look and liked what we saw.

So the next January, Ruth and I and Shirley and Milton went to the Helsinki Fashion Fair to buy clothing for our stores. It became an annual trip for many years. We introduced interesting new brands to our store but the absolute winner was Luhta, a skiwear line that cane out of the Finnish army mountain patrol ski suits.

The fabric was warm but also light, very easy and comfortable. Luhta's design team made their ski wear in a wide range of bright colors—yellow, orange, red, light blue, pink, and lots of white; and they made styles for men, women and children.

I asked our salesman why the line wasn't available in the big U.S. stores. His answer, "The better departments stores we would sell to, such as Saks and Neiman Marcus, need larger quantities than we could supply. If we filled their orders, we could not ship to our customers in Finland, Germany, France. etc. Gordon's is a perfect size store for us to have as a customer." And Luhta was perfect for us!

We were accompanied by the Blumbergs on one of our Finnish excursions and learned from Marty about the country's world-class architects. On another visit, the Gordons and Raphels had the good fortune to tour the Iittala plant where their tableware products were created and even met some of the designers.

The whole Finnish experience left us with great admiration for the country and their attention to design, especially in Helsinki. We are glad the Whitmans shared the Fashion Fair experience with us; and also our nephew Jeffrey Gordon, who, at the time, was developing a young men's shop in Gordon's.

New Jersey Retailer of the Year

Every year the New Jersey Retail Merchants Association chooses the New Jersey Retailer of the Year.

When I submitted an application after Gordon's Alley was developed, I put any thought of winning on the back burner. After all, Atlantic City was not known for its retailing. The economy was in trouble with 11 percent unemployment. Retailers were leaving the city at a rate of 10 percent every year. These were not encouraging statistics to judges.

But despite these demographics (or because of them), I succeeded that year in winning the title. Of course, the success of

Gordon's Alley was a determining factor in choosing me as "New Jersey's Retailer of the Year."

The ceremony was held at the Great Gorge Hotel in northern New Jersey. The New Jersey Retail Merchants' president Nathan Goodman introduced me. I received a standing ovation from the audience of 120 that included fellow Atlantic City merchants, professionals, and civic leaders, who had charted a plane from Atlantic City's Bader Field. Also, there was my mother and father, Ruth and our partner family, Shirley and Milton Gordon.

Peter Goodman, in his introduction of me, repeated the part of my birth that quoted my mother saying, "No doctor or lawyer for our son. He is destined to be a successful businessman."

Looking back, I don't remember if I was composed enough to thank all the people who made it possible for me to receive the honor of being "New Jersey's Retailer of the Year," but I hope I said, "It would not have been possible without my partners: Ruth, Shirley, and Milton; our wonderful, hard working staff; and all the brave and talented retailers who joined us in the adventure of Gordon's Alley."

Our staff at Gordon's, Fellow Retailers and Our Suppliers

I don't know any store that could have a better or more loyal staff than we enjoyed. There are too many names to mention from our nearly 50 years in business but they served our customers with honesty and professionalism. We enjoyed meetings, dinners and family events together. We take our hats off to all of them.

Because I was involved with politics and civic duties that kept me away many hours from my immediate store responsibility— the men's shop—I have to mention Eddie Barron, the manager of the men's store. He gave me the peace of mind to know the men's business was managed properly. It could not have been in better hands.

We showed our appreciation to our staff for several years by closing our stores over a long weekend and taking them all on mini-vacations. Trips included visits to Disneyland, Nashville. and Vermont. The trip to Vermont was interesting because we went by a "high roller" bus with great amenities. It was fun for me because I spent summers at my grandmother's in Vermont and knew all the best places to stop. In addition, with gratitude to Eddie for the sales he created and special connection with customers, we sent him and his family to vacation in Honolulu, Hawaii.

There were three wonderful ladies—Margaret, Thelma, and Mae—who were responsible for our households at various times. They made it possible for Shirley and Ruth to spend so much time downstairs in the stores. The Gordons and Raphels and their children remember them fondly and with love.

I need to mention Tony Tabasso, our window trimmer. He and his brother Michael gave Gordon's the professional and artistic look to our windows with style and originality. They also decorated the store interior for Christmas and special occasions. We talked about each trim in advance, then Tony gave us our marching orders—what we needed to buy or borrow for his trim. He made us work hard but the results were worthwhile, as there always a theme or story to the settings and not just dressed-up mannequins.

Then there were the retailers who joined with us to make Gordon's Alley work as a full shopping experience. I'll mention some of them here. Fabers, owned by Skippy and Bud Faber, a gift store of exceptional quality and taste. Ruth Ann Saul and Ann Bressler, with their books and unusual greeting cards, brought us many customers. Our former employee, Harry Bachen, along with Michael Eattock, opened Bachen & Eattock's Bootery as did Beverly Ward with Bonne Nuit, whose store featured special lingerie. Shirley and Milt's son Norman opened the popular Alley Deli. Suzie Boots ran the most exciting junior store in town, later bought and managed by Patty Nugent. Mike Rozet developed Le

Grand Fromage, a cheese shop and restaurant. Mike, a great chef and jazz musician, brought an art ambience to the Alley. There were many other retailers inside the main Gordon's store, down the Alley and inside the Garage that added excitement to the retail mix.

Also, from our many years in business, we made countless friends with owners and sales representatives of the branded and individually produced merchandise we featured in our stores. Many of these sales people and executives became friends, attending our celebrations, becoming involved in our promotions, including "Little Miss Atlantic City" scholarships and attendance at the final night of the contest. Several of them even helped us out on our New Year's Day sales.

One special company to highlight is Anna Modeller of Sweden. We had originally discovered this women's clothing line in our annual trek to the Finnish Fashion Fair in Helsinki. We did well with the line, struck up a friendship with the owner, and visited her and her family in Malmö, Sweden. Then came an idea. How about an exclusive Anna Modeller fashion show sponsored by Gordon's in Atlantic City? We held it in the pre-casino hotel, Haddon Hall, invitation only. It was an elegant event with professional models and original Swedish music.

Or how about the Ralph Lauren exclusive Gordon's fashion show held at the polo grounds outside of Atlantic City with lunch for the invited guests and the latest RL fashions?

From the sublime to the ridiculous: When we were still just a children's store and struggling, Marvin Manton, a salesman from Fieldstone Clothing, a boy's coat line, lent us his room at a New York hotel so that Ruth and I and Shirley and Milt (the four of us in one room) could spend New Year's Eve in New York and see the fabulous musical, "My Fair Lady."

50 years of great memories!

The Gordon's Gold Card

In Dale Carnegie's book, *How to Win Friends and Influence People,* he stresses the importance of a person's name in establishing a close relationship.

A number of years ago we saw the marketing world use that tenet—the importance of a person's name—in the start of Frequent Flyer programs to create loyalty between customers and airlines.

American Airlines was among the first to offer their best customers a Frequent Flyer program with special bonuses for customers who selected that airline for future travel plans. The rest of the airlines followed their lead.

Then the major hotels and department stores encouraged their best customers to join their Frequent Buyer Clubs, as did many other retail businesses including supermarkets.

We were always looking for ways to have our best customers shop more often.

But who were they? We turned to our computer to seek names of individuals who spent $1,000 or more a year with us. When we established a list of our best customers, we were ready to begin the work of creating the Gordon's Gold Card. This tied in perfectly with my philosophy that "it is far, far easier to sell more to a current customer than to sell a new customer."

First, we needed a letter to inform the customers on the list of the benefits in being selected for the Gordon's Gold Card. We reviewed the many letters we compiled from all the airlines, hotels, and department stores asking us to be a member of their Frequent Flyer/Buyer programs.

To our surprise, almost every letter had one identical sentence repeated in every solicitation. Here it is:

"Your association with (name of their company) and your annual volume of business places you in a unique group which requires and appreciates special recognition."

Couldn't have said it better myself.

So I used a similar message in a personal letter to each customer selected to be a member of the Gordon's Gold Card program. I also included a questionnaire to better serve them and some of the benefits they would receive.

The short questionnaire asked for their birthday as well as their spouse's birth date. (Both the recipient and the spouse would receive a $10 gift certificate a few weeks before their birthday to spend in our men's or women's shop.)

The questionnaire also asked and gave us information on the different shops they patronized in Gordon's Alley, as well as what advertising media was most read or heard.

A complimentary "lunch package" was included in the letter to Gold Card members to enjoy: monthly gift certificates for one year for lunch at the Alley Deli Restaurant—a $60.00 value.

More than 300 questionnaires were returned!

WHAT THIS MEANT: We had more than 300 customers we targeted who accepted our invitation and whom we could continue to target with special benefits and rewards.

What this also gave us was information to increase our sales and another favorite tenet of mine: "Find out what the customers want...and give it to them!"

The Gordon's Gold Card was successful. We learned to use the sales information to reward our customers on their brand preferences such as a whole series of promotions with Ralph Lauren purchases. The card remained valuable until we decided to end our retail business.

Chapter Three
Promotions

My First Promotion:
The Helena Rubinstein Direct Mailer

I gave a seminar on direct marketing in the New York Hilton Hotel to the National Retail Merchants Association at their annual convention. When I finished, a young man with a British accent spoke to me about a direct mail campaign created by Helena Rubenstein, the cosmetic company where he worked.

"We offered a direct mail campaign to major department stores across the country to send their customers that included a coupon for a free gift of a new Helena Rubenstein product." But, he continued, "The results were very disappointing."

His next question stirred my interest. Would I review the mailer with their marketing director and give him my views on what I thought they were doing wrong? I agreed and set a time for the meeting. A week later I met with their marketing director, examined the mailer and in a few minutes I discovered the problem.

The mailer awarded the customer a free gift from Helena Rubenstein. As a retailer, I want the credit for whatever a manufacturer is offering my customer. The offer should come from me, the retailer, not the manufacturer. I must receive the credit and good will when a mailer is sent to my list.

I suggested I would take the mailing piece home and return in a week with my ideas for a reworked version. They agreed.

Back in my office I rewrote new copy for the mailer. The giver of the free gift was changed from Helena Rubenstein to the retailer. I also pointed out the word "coupon" is what people cut out of their newspaper to save money for food shopping. Instead, I used the words 'gift certificate" and made it clear the "gift" was from the retailer, not from Helena Rubenstein. I gave the corrected copy to my artist who created a new sophisticated mailer.

Then I wondered, "What would make the customer return to the store again AFTER she used the gift certificate?" The store had the customer's name and address, so I created a second mailer to send to each customer after she used the first gift certificate. This new mailer was a booklet with four gift certificates for the customer to use—one for each succeeding week. Each certificate had the customer's name so she would see the gift certificate was exclusively for her. I was ready to set up my new meeting with the advertising director. Now I faced a new problem: how much do I charge Helena Rubenstein for my work on these two mailers? I first asked my artist how much he wanted for his design. He said $400. I figured I would add $600 for my copy. That was a total of $1,000.

Then I showed the layout for the two new mailers to an advertising friend, asking if he thought price sounded fair. He said, "You've got to be kidding. Your price is much too low." I replied that the figure was $300 more than I charged a local stationery account for a mailer that was just as good. "But this is a national account," he countered. "They will think a mailer with that low a price cannot be first-rate."

He gave me the example: "When a doctor walks into the patient's hospital room he looks at the x-rays and says, "Don't operate...and then sends you a bill for $500. You might call him and say, 'That's a lot of money for only saying two words.' The doctor could then answer, 'But it took me ten years to learn when to say those two words.' You're not charging your customer only for the time you spent putting their two new mailers together, but for your knowledge and work to accumulate the right words to use."

I went to New York the next week for the scheduled meeting with Helena Rubenstein's marketing director. I arrived at his office and gave my prepared speech. "Okay, I've brought you my ideas to increase the response of your mailer. I'm not going to explain what I did. Instead I want you to make believe you are the person receiving this mailer. You open it up..."

He opened the large envelope and the smaller envelope with my reworked mailer dropped out. He picked it up, read it, and then said, "I see you discovered the problem. The mailer should be coming from the store, not us, the manufacturer."

"There's more," I said, and then went through with him the follow-up mailer with the gift certificates to bring the customer back to the store four more times. He said, "Excellent idea and great design. I'll buy them both. When can you bring me camera-ready material?" I hesitated in order not to appear too anxious. Then I softly replied, "How about in two weeks?"

He said that was okay, but wanted to go over pricing. And then he added the sentence that sent my head to the clouds, "Which price are you giving me first, the corrected mailer or the follow-up?" Now came the moment of decision. I decided to offer the price of the corrected mailer first. "How does $1,500 sound to you?" I asked. "That's fine," he said. "The follow-up mailer has a lot more work. How about $2,500 for that one? Just send me a bill. Is that all right with you?"

Is that all right with me? I had originally planned to charge $1,000 for the work. It turned out to be worth a lot more. I left the marketing director's office and ran down Fifth Avenue five feet in the air.

Back in my office at home, I remembered the story of a

young optometrist: After graduating college, he joined his father in business and asked, "How do I know how much to charge for new glasses?" "Simple," said the father. "When you fit the glasses to the customer and they ask you how much the glasses cost you say, 'Twenty dollars.' If they don't blink, add 'For each glass.' If they still don't blink, you say 'And the cost of the frame is'..."

Clarabell the Clown

We needed exciting promotions to create interest and publicity and have Gordon's talked about throughout our selling area. Our first event was to have a clown—who couldn't talk—visit the store.

When children watched television in the late afternoon, after school, their favorite program—before Sesame Street and Mister Roger's Neighborhood—was the Howdy Doody Show on NBC. The host was Buffalo Bob Smith who introduced Howdy Doody and the other players on his daily program including Howdy's best pal Clarabell the clown.

Howdy Doody was a wooden puppet with a freckled face and tousled hair who wore blue jeans, cowboy boots, plaid shirt and a bandana.

Here's how popular Howdy Doody was: when Buffalo Bob put up Howdy Doody as a candidate for U.S. President in 1948, Howdy received more votes than Henry Wallace, who was running on the Progressive Party ticket.

At the show's peak, its audience averaged between 12 and 14 million people making it to the top ten nationally-rated shows.

The children's favorite character on the show was Clarabell the clown. His costume was a baggy body length green and white zebra striped coverall. Kids didn't care he didn't talk. They loved his beeping rubber horn (shades of Harpo Marx) and seltzer bottle that he squirted at his pals, resulting in peals of laughter from children in the studio audience as well as the young school set everywhere, sitting rapt in front of their black and white TVs.

At that time, our most popular clothing item for boys and girls was a zip front overall called Kwiki that made it easy for children to put on and take off. So when I read an article in our trade journal that Macy's had Clarabell appear in person for a Kwiki overall promotion, a marketing light bulb went off. The light bulb exploded when I read further and learned a huge crowd of children came to see him and to buy the new Kwiki Clarabell print overall.

Wait a minute! If Macy's had him live in person at their store, why couldn't I have Clarabell come to Gordon's? I contacted our Kwiki salesperson and said I wanted to have Clarabell come to our store. I was referred to the sales manager. His reply, "You have to purchase the same quantity as Macy's if you want Clarabell at Gordon's." "What is that amount?" I asked gingerly. He said, "We need an order of 24 dozen of the Clarabell screen printed overalls in one color."

Wow! 24 dozen. That meant 288 pair of these special overalls This presented a problem, We never bought more than 100 pairs of Kwiki overalls for an entire season and only in assorted solid colors. Could we sell 288 overalls in one color screen printed with Clarabell's face? Yes. I was positive. My partners also had their own positive response: "NO!"

I persevered, and we agreed to buy the quantity of overalls that would guarantee Clarabell's appearance. I designed a full-page ad for the local paper announcing the date of Clarabell's in-person appearance at Gordon's.

We asked the mayor for two or three motorcycle patrolman to escort our car when we welcomed Clarabell in Atlantic City and subsequently brought him to the store. The mayor agreed with one condition. His two grandsons were fans of Clarabell. If they could sit in the convertible car next to Clarabell, the mayor would supply the motorcycle police escorts. I quickly agreed!

Clarabell arrived secretly several hours ahead of the announced time so that he could change into his costume at my in-laws' small hotel. We then piled into our convertible car (rented for the day), picked up the mayor's grandsons, drove to the train station where his announced arrival took place, and took off with the motorcycle escorts and horns blowing. Crowds of children and parents filled the sidewalks, cheering and applauding. The kids waved to Clarabell, who honked his horn and waved back.

I turned to my partners sitting in the car and gave the final marketing proclamation: "If this promotion turns out to be as successful as I think it will be, we'll all share the credit. And if it fails, we'll all share the loss." They agreed.

We arrived at our store and could not believe the crowds. Hundreds of children and parents were waiting for us! The motorcycle cops jumped off their vehicles to help with crowd control. The children and parents poured into our store to meet Clarabell and receive his signed autographed pictures.

We did not sell out of overalls that day. And yes, there was pilferage, but it wasn't until a few weeks later that we realized the lasting power of an in-store celebrity's live appearance. As children walked by the front of our store, we heard them telling their parents, "Look. This is where Clarabell lives!"

Mission accomplished. The publicity and entertainment value of Clarabell, having Gordon's name stand out in front of the other retailers, more than compensated for the expense.

Nothing else could possibly draw that many people...so I thought. I hadn't realized the tremendous appeal of another television and movie celebrity. He came to Gordon's and attracted three times the amount of customers and potential customers. His name: Mickey Mouse.

Mickey Mouse

*W*ho's the leader of the club
That's made for you and me?
M-I-C-K-E-Y M-O U-S-E

Hey there! Hi there! Ho there!
You're as welcome as can be
M-I-C-K-E-Y M-O-U-S E....etc.

Howdy Doody met his Waterloo in Mickey Mouse.

When "The Mickey Mouse Club" went on television a half hour before "Howdy Doody" weekday afternoons, the stringed marionettes and costumed vaudevillians of Doodyville suddenly looked dowdy and awfully tired compared with The Mickey Mouse Club. "The MM Club" was modern and pert, featuring talented young people mirroring the ages of the kids in the TV audiences and connecting with them. The ratings were over the top.

A new marketing idea clicked. If Mickey Mouse ratings beat Clarabell on TV, how do we have Mickey come "in person" to our store? The answer to that to that question was complicated. There were no manufacturers of merchandise to help with the cost and the negotiations. Mickey was in demand all over the country. Could we have him come to Gordon's in Atlantic City? Well...as my Uncle Julius used to say, "It don't 'hoit' to ask."

The fear of rejection often makes the task of asking difficult. I thought about a very successful real estate salesman in our community. He had a phenomenal rate of securing mortgage loans from local banks. I once asked him the secret of his success. His answer: "I never ask a question unless I know the answer is 'yes.'"

That memory triggered a solution. In the international selling seminars I gave to businesses, I always advised the attendees to make sure you are ready to supply—to anyone you are selling—

the answer to the question "What's in it for me?" The Disney people knew what was it it for us. Having Mickey Mouse in person at our store would mean increased customers, sales, and unbelievable publicity–but what was in it for them?

We contacted the promotion people at Disney. We told them we would do the following:

a. Put together a giant Mickey Mouse float for the Christmas parade in Atlantic City.

b. Build a Mouse House in our store to hold "Mickey" clothing and accessories.

c. People could register for a drawing for a top prize—air travel and accommodations to Disney World—and several prizes for merchandise in our Mouse House.

They were impressed and gave us their commitment to participate, including the airline tickets and rooms at Disney World saying, "Your ideas sound like one hell of a promotional program."

But what about Mickey Mouse? Would he be here in person?

We soon found out—there was no Mickey coming, but, instead, a Mickey Mouse costume for one of our employees to wear, providing the employee was less than five feet three inches.

One of our female salesladies, Toni Riccardi, volunteered to wear the costume and be "our Mickey." Since she was the right height, we submitted her application and agreed to the very specific instructions—while wearing the outfit, do not talk to anyone (as Mickey does not talk); smile and shake hands with everyone; give out gifts to children (which we purchased for the event). We co-signed the agreement form along with Toni, sent it to the Disney promotion office and soon received the costume.

Gordon's was now ready for Mickey to visit our store!

As the big event neared, we carefully reviewed our plans for the Mickey Mouse parade and checked the delivery date for orders of Disney merchandise to fill our Mouse House. Knowing the importance of the event to our business, we added other

elements to the promotion:
- A free photo with Mickey for any child accompanied by an adult
- A children's art contest, open to any student from the local elementary schools using "The Wonderful World of Disney" theme under the supervision and judging by area art teachers
- A gift for each child (with an adult) when they left the store

The crowds of parents and children began to line up on the streets for the parade and then dashed to our store for their free picture with Mickey and shop the Mouse House for souvenirs. The crowed was controlled by two experienced off-duty policemen we hired for the event. At the end of the day, we estimated that several thousand children and parents came to Gordon's—nearly twice the crowd of the Clarabell promotion.

It was the biggest promotion in terms of people and business in the history of our store. Could this record ever be broken? We doubted it. However, we never anticipated our next promotion. A promotion for only three hours. but in those three hours we did more business than in any two weeks of the year!

I wrote the story for several magazines and inspired other stores to create the same promotion. It is our next story and it was—"The New Year's Day Sale."

The New Year's Day Sale

It was time to put together the advertising for our annual end-of-the-year sale of fall and winter clothing. The problem was that every other retailer in our town was also putting together advertising for their fall and winter sale. What could we do that was different, exciting, and bring crowds of customers to our store?

One evening during dinner, I said to Ruth, Shirley, and Milton, "I have a great idea for our fall and winter sale. Let's have it on New Year's Day! The response was immediate...and negative. Shirley said, "Couldn't this have waited till after dinner? Milton added, "At least until dessert and coffee." My wife Ruth concluded, "Everyone will be home watching the football games on TV."

Other arguments followed:

"Most people will still be recovering from the previous night's festivities."

"Do you know what the weather will be like that day? Probably rain or snow and, with reduced holiday services, traffic conditions will be impossible."

And...

"All the other stores in town will be closed so that cuts down the regular street traffic we could have on a regular shopping day."

The final one—

"If it's such a great idea, how come nobody else ever did it?"

I finally prevailed and designed a mailer to be sent to the 3,000 customers on our mailing list with the sale time and date boldly listed as 12:00 noon to 3:00 pm, January 1.

That mailer quickly prompted a slew of customer phone calls—most of the callers asking the same question, "Did you make a mistake? Did you mean the sale starts on January 11, not January 1?" I assured these customers the date was correct and encouraged them to come early for best selection.

New Year's Day: The staff and family opened the store early to straighten stock, check counters for cash, credit card slips (before instant scanning) and bags/boxes. About 10:30 am, my nephew Steven Gordon called our attention to both the front and back door (entrance from our parking lot). We looked and saw hundreds of people lined up waiting for the store to open.

Our next move was to phone the police station and ask for help. We hired off-duty policemen to handle the crowd. Three policemen arrived in time for us to open the doors at 12:00 noon as scheduled. Staff and family were at both entrances welcoming the now thousands of people, stretching around the block, to our first New Year's Day sale.

The sale lasted for three hours. We ushered out the last customers at our scheduled closing time of 3:00 pm. Our nephew Steve then went with one of the off-duty policemen to deposit the day's receipts in the night deposit slot of our bank.

When the result of our three hour New Year's Day sale was tallied, we discovered we had done more business during those three hours than we had done in any three day history of our business!

I wrote about this successful promotion in my several columns for retail trade magazines and spoke about the promotion in seminars I gave to business audiences around the world. We received letters and phone calls from many of the retailers who read or heard the idea of having a New Year's Day sale, thanking us for the positive results they also had.

At the same time, we tried to convince local merchants to join us and have a sale on New Year's Day. Most of them replied with the familiar negative answer we heard at our dining room table, "Are you crazy? Who wants to shop on New Year's Day?" Ten years later every store on the main street was open for business on January 1. The success of our sale year after year could not be ignored.

What we did for this promotion to increase sales every year was twofold:

1. We did not take for granted that customers would show up, especially since it was on a day we were normally closed and opened for a limited time. We kept broadcasting the information. We did it then with direct mail, radio spots, newspaper ads and phone contacts. Today, we would have included televison and, with the Internet, we would have added emails and notices on our website and other wireless devices.

2. Each year we added a marketing strategy or changed our mailing piece enough to create newness and build excitement for this important sale.

a. One year we printed for each customer on our mailing list their "lucky number" next to their address. Inside the mailer, we told them to bring their lucky number with them to the sale to check it against the winning numbers posted at each cash register to see how much money they won when they came to the store. We stressed that everybody was a winner!

• The winning numbers were listed on a large poster next to the cash registers with values ranging from $2 to $100. The customers could apply what they won towards their sale purchases.

• The majority of the lucky numbers' winning amount was $2. But other prizes ranged from $5 to $100. Whenever anyone won $25 to $100, we rang a loud cowbell (purchased at a farm auction in Vermont) and turned on the PA system to announce the name of the winner and the amount.

• Customers loved the theatrics...and also checked their numbers carefully.

b. Another year we used a replica of a theatrical bill as our direct mail theme. With the mailer, we sent two "tickets" for admission to the sale with the customer's name printed on each ticket. Of course, no one needed a ticket to come to our sale; but we thought it was fun and it worked with our theme. Besides, what customer would think you had to have a ticket for a sale?

But...

A few days after the mailer was sent, the phone rang. "This is Jane Smith from Chelsea Heights. I just received your advertisement for your New Year's Day Sale with two tickets. Here's why I'm calling. I have an aunt and a cousin coming in for the weekend and I was wondering, could I have two more tickets?"

I answered, "Let me get this straight. You want me to

send you two more tickets for two more people to come and spend money in my store. Is that right?"

"Yes," she said.

"I can handle that!" I answered.

In Case of a Tie,
the Winner is Wembley!

"How's business?" I asked Tim, the salesman from Wembley ties, as he was showing his new fall tie line to Eddie, the manager of my men's store and myself. "Could be better," he replied. "The competition is tough." As we laid out our tie choices, Tim wrote up the order. Afterwards, Tim handed me a copy of the order and said, "You picked the winners!"

A light bulb went off in my head. "Tim, I have a suggestion for you to take back to your bosses to increase business. Have a contest among all your retailers for the best advertising of Wembley ties. Create response and excitement by giving great prizes to the store with the best promotion."

"What would make a retailer like yourself want to enter a contest?" Tim asked me. I thought about it and answered, "An all paid vacation to New Orleans where Wembley ties are made might make an appropriate prize." Then I thought about what would make me return to New Orleans and gave Tim a rundown of what to include:

- A weekend in New Orleans at a top hotel in the French Quarter
- A tour of the French Quarter
- Beignets and café au lait at Café Du Monde in Jackson Square
- Dinners at famous New Orleans restaurants, including Antoine's
- Breakfast at Brennan's

I told Tim, "It can't miss. Every retailer will want to win. And think of all the Wembley ties they will promote and sell!"

A few weeks later Tim called to tell me the president of Wembley liked the contest idea and decided to go ahead with it. "Great," I said. "And what's my reward for coming up with the idea?" A long pause on the telephone and then Tim answered, "You can enter the contest."

I met with my partners and gave them the news. "Guess what. We're all going to New Orleans for a vacation as the national contest winners of the best promotion of Wembley ties with all our expenses paid for by the Wembley Company." Before anyone could ask how much we had to spend on the promotion, I quickly outlined my ideas for winning.

"We'll start with a special 'Wembley Week.' Customers can bring in any old tie in their wardrobe and receive a credit of three dollars towards any new Wembley tie they purchase. Customers can also sign up to win a Wembley sweepstakes for $50 worth of Wembley ties. 'Miss Wembley' will give out the entry blanks for the sweepstakes as customers come into our store." (Miss Wembley didn't exist before the contest. Later, we offered the title and wining sash to one of our attractive saleswomen. She agreed, saying, "This is the first title I've ever won." We all applauded.)

But there was still something missing...something so exciting that would make the Wembley judges unanimously say, "This is the winner!" Since one of the judges was Sidney Pulitzer, the owner of Wembley, we sought information about him. Did he have any special hobbies? Yes, he did—thoroughbred horses. Another light bulb went off in my head.

What if we could have a horse race named "The Wembley" at the local Atlantic City Raceway. Instead of a garland of roses given to the winning horse, would the track officials allow a special ten foot long Wembley tie to be placed around the horse's neck in addition to the trophy?

The track officials agreed, with the caveat that Gordon's pay $100 for the winning trophy and supply the tie. We quickly agreed. The Racing Form would call the race "The Gordon's Alley Wembley Trot." And in exchange for our promoting the Atlantic City Raceway in our ads, we were allowed to give away a free dinner for two at the track's quality restaurant.

We also came up with an exciting radio ad. We hired the track announcer, who had a recognized voice, to advertise the race as if it was actually happening. The radio audience heard the sound of horses' hooves pounding away in the background as the broadcaster says, "As they make the first turn we see the Wembley horse leading the pack." After a few minutes, he announces excitedly, "The winning horse is Wembley and, as the winner, he receives a ten foot Wembley tie made just for him. But in case of a tie..." (Silence)

A few days before the race we came up with another idea. We found out the track coach at a local college, Larry James, was a former winner of an Olympic silver medal. We arranged to have him run a special race with the Wembley horse the day of the Wembley Trot. We included the announcement in our closing advertisements.

The evening of the event, the Olympic athlete came in first! James received a special Wembley tie which he showed off to the crowd as he made a winning lap around the track. The crowd loved the show. And the sports writers of the area newspapers wrote great feature stories on the race.

Promotion, promotion, promotion is the answer to any event's success.

We put together a portfolio of what we did for the contest and mailed our entry to Wembley the next week. The letter from Sidney Pulitzer arrived a short time later saying we won!

P.S. We had a great time in New Orleans!

The Day We Gave a Parade and Nobody Came

It was Stanley Marcus of Neiman Marcus department store fame who gave us an idea for a great promotion...turning our store into a celebration of a travel destination that delights customers.

Of course, Stanley Marcus was an original who headed a major retail company with the means to put on major promotions. He selected different countries around the world; his buyers bought large quantities of clothing and products made in those countries; his store and display windows featured displays of the particular country; the imported merchandise was featured in every department; all this in a "Fortnight" (two week) promotion.

If it worked for Neiman Marcus (it did, it did), why not have it work for Gordon's as well?

I had just returned from a speaking job in Ireland. I had toured the southern countryside, traveled the Ring of Kerry and kissed the stone at Blarney Castle to insure the success of Gordon's future. It was natural for us to select Ireland for our own Fortnight promotion. It was following my basic rule for having a successful promotion: "Steal Any Idea Thou Can and Claim It For Thy Very Own."

We assembled our staff and told them the plan. Our own Irish promotion would begin on Saint Patrick's Day. It was just a month away—perfect timing.

We would carry Irish merchandise to sell in our stores including hand made Aran sweaters, Waterford crystal and other famous Irish brands.

To heighten excitement, I would make arrangements to have the first Saint Patrick's Day Parade in Atlantic City's history. Parades are fun and exciting. They bring out crowds. A Grand Marshal would lead the parade that started at City Hall and marched the ten blocks to our stores in Gordon's Alley. Even Stanley Marcus never had a parade!

But first we decided to tie in with a traditional promotion—Atlantic City's annual black tie dinner sponsored by the local chapter of the Sons of Saint Patrick. As a speaker, I offered to take responsibility for the keynote speaker at the dinner (which was the night before our proposed parade). The president of the chapter graciously accepted my offer. When I suggested the Irish Consul, he was in full agreement.

Next, I met with the mayor and told him our plans for an Irish promotion. He thought it was good publicity for the city and asked how he could help. I asked him to write to the Irish Consul and invite him to be the speaker for the Saint Patrick's Day dinner. I also asked the mayor for his endorsement of Gordon's Saint Patrick's Day Parade. He agreed.

The Irish Consul replied to the mayor's letter that he was already committed. Would Atlantic City consider having a Vice Consul? All parties to the promotion agreed it was fine. The Mayor sent our acceptance and appreciation of having the Vice Consul in our city for Saint Patrick's Day.

Gordon's immediately hired a local theatre group's art designer to create "thatched roofs" on the front of the stores facing the parade route so we'd look authentic old Irish. Next we contacted Ireland's official airline, Aer Lingus. Would they give us two round trip tickets to Ireland to give away in a sweepstakes as part of our Irish promotion if we credited Aer Lingus in our newspaper ads and a mailer sent to 10,000 customers? They agreed.

During the next few days we had appropriate events: Irish musical entertainment in our main store; Irish stew and corned beef & cabbage lunches in our restaurants; Irish ready-to-wear in our men's, women's and children's shops; and Irish specialty foods in the gift shop.

The Irish Vice Consul arrived on schedule the day before the start of the parade and we greeted him with the Gaelic welcoming phrase we all had carefully memorized, "Céad Míle Fáilte" (a hundred thousand welcomes). We then turned him over to a local Irish politician friend who volunteered to show him the sights of Atlantic City. Little did we know it included introducing him to all the local Irish bartenders.

That night we went to the Sons of Saint Patrick's dinner at our top local hotel and noticed the Irish Vice Consul was not seated at the head table. He was still not there even after everyone was served.

Feeling responsible, I offered to check on him. I went to his room. I knocked hard. No answer. I persuaded the hotel manager to send up the bellhop with a key. He opened the door and we saw the Vice Consul, sleeping soundly in his bed and obviously inebriated.

We woke him up; had him shower and change into his formal clothes; gave him coffee; and escorted him to the front table at the banquet. He smiled and waved to the audience as though they were his friends for many years.

I introduced him. He went to the podium, looked over the crowd, and gave his speech... in Gaelic! He assumed he was back in Dublin among a friendly Irish crowd who loved hearing those Gaelic sounds.

The Atlantic City audience was mesmerized for a different reason. Most in the room thought it was a comedy routine... waiting to hear him revert to plain old English. I knew differently and quietly slipped from my chair to under the table. My wife whispered, "Sit up. It's okay. Someone told him to end it." He did. But he added a few jokes (yes, in Gaelic) and laughed heartily after each one. When he finally finished, the audience gave him an embarrassed applause. It was not a fortuitous beginning to our Irish promotion.

The next day the Irish Vice Consul had recovered sufficiently to host the official flag raising ceremony at City Hall. We had a pleasant lunch together and waved goodbye.

We were now convinced whatever could go wrong did go wrong. After all, the next day was the *piece de resistance*. What could possibly go wrong with a parade?

The Day of the Parade:

Employees of Air Lingus showed up to help handle the crowds. The Mayor had the police clear the streets for the ten-block march. The big parade attraction was the winning band of the famous Philadelphia Mummers. Their costumes were feathered, jeweled, and gaudy. They played their saxophones, banjos, and glockenspiels as the dancers strutted down the street. I fulfilled my dream as the Grand Marshall of a parade, leading the Mummers along the parade route.

AND NO ONE CAME. A few scattered people...a few cars beeped in approval. As the leader of the Mummers band said to me as they boarded their private bus to return home, "Was this the dress rehearsal? If not, where were all the people?"

What we did learn? Just this: not all promotions work. It's important to do enough of them to come out on the plus side.

Another important lesson: keep promotions to a short leash. Four hours? One day? Two days at the most. Most stores don't have the ideas, the manpower, or the budget for longer events.

LEE JEANS: Absolute-LEE, Positive-LEE, Defiknit-LEE

One morning, the mail brought me a notice that Lee Jeans was sponsoring a contest for retailers who sold their jean line.

The Lee Jean Company was introducing double knit jeans —a new product that had a denim feel and look, but was knitted instead of woven. Several other jean manufacturers were also coming out with a similar product. Lee wanted their retailers to enter a contest showing how they marketed and sold Lee jeans by differentiating them from the competition. In other words, advertising Lee's USP (unique selling proposition).

Rules of the contest included submission of:

- photos of displays
- newspaper ads
- radio script
- other promotional tools—whatever the retailer did to promote the new double knit jean from Lee.

I looked at the prizes—a trip for two to London including tickets to a rock concert. London was interesting but the rock concert had no appeal. What really had me panting to win was the offer of a full-page ad from our store (Gordon's) in Esquire magazine if we were the contest winner.

That started me on the entry.

I began by putting together two strategies—one for "sound" (radio) and one for "look" (print) to promote the new Lee jeans in our men's and prep shops.

But there was an element needed that would make our ads stand out—our own USP.

I began by working with the word "LEE" since that was the brand name. I thought about all the words beginning with "lee" such as leech, leek, leery, leer, even leeward. Not much there and most of it negative. How about a suffix using "lee" to end words? Since the new jeans were knit, I played around with the word "knit" and, out of somewhere came "definite." Wait—that could be "defi-knit-LEE."

Thunder roared! Lightning struck! The room was ablaze with color! That one simple suffix "ly" spelled instead "LEE" was the key to the promotion. From there, in a few minutes, the rest of the words came pouring out:

How do they fit? Perfect-LEE.

How do they feel? Comfortable-LEE.

How do they look? Handsome-LEE.

What is their wardrobe status? Basic-LEE.

Are Lee jeans right for you? Absolute-LEE.

Are you sure? Positive-LEE.

The slogan was there. Next—the art.

Our artist was excellent—perfect for the job. The problem

was he was tremendously talented and completely unreliable.

He came to my office and we discussed the design. The decision was to do something simple. Since one of the prizes was a full-page ad in Esquire, why not have great art of a man wearing LEE jeans standing in front of a replica of a cover of Esquire magazine with the new headline "How do LEE's new jeans fit? PerfectLEE!" Simple. Dramatic Effective.

What was still needed: something for the young woman that also bought Lee jeans. The artist did a sketch of an attractive young girl wearing Lee knit jeans with a tiny cat in her arms. This was the headline: "How do LEE knits fit? Purrrrrrrfect LEE."

Since this talented artist of ours had a habit of not showing up to work on a regular basis, we had to keep him close to have the art in time for the contest. We solved that problem by locking him and his art supplies in an empty apartment above our store until he finished the work. We checked on him during the day and brought him delicious catered meals. We promised to free him after he finished the six ads we needed for the contest entry and to give him a cash bonus. Since he needed the money, he agreed. Two days later he gave us the finished ads. We unlocked the apartment door and gave him the promised bonus. He was happy and so were we. The finished art was fantastic!

We took the ads, the radio scripts, the window display photos, our entry— mailed them...and waited.

The letter arrived a few weeks later saying we won!

Since our competition were major department stores and large specialty shops across the U.S., we were really proud and excited. As an extra bonus, the four partners from Gordon's were awarded an all-expense-paid trip to Cincinnati for the World Series.

The local newspapers gave us great publicity and *Advertising Age*, the trade magazine for the advertising industry, wrote up the winning entry with a picture of the "PurrrrfectLEE" ad. That Esquire publicity resulted in phone calls from across the country as well as local customers who wanted to buy Lee's new knit jeans.

The round trip to London came at a time when we had other plans, so our two teen-age daughters took our place. When they returned, we asked them what they liked most: The English Bobbies? Thechanging of the guard at Buckingham Palace? The Tower of London? What?

Their answer: "The rock concert!"

ObviousLee.

"Here She Is...Little Miss Atlantic City"

Every community is known for something...or should be. In Troy, New York, where I grew up, my town was known as the home of "Uncle Sam," the fictional character with the white goatee, top hat, and patriotic red, white, and blue clothes.

How did "Uncle Sam" become a symbol of the U.S.?

At the time of the American Revolutionary War, many supplies were shipped from a depot in Troy, New York to the American army warehouses. One of the suppliers was Sam Wilson, a meat packer, affectionately known as "Uncle Sam." He stamped those initials—U.S.—on the sides of the barrels holding his provisions. The soldiers thought the initialed letters meant the contents came officially from the United States Government— U.S. And the legend took off from there.

When I married an Atlantic City girl and we went into business there with my sister-in-law and brother-in-law, I soon recognized that Atlantic City's iconic image was the annual Miss America Pageant.

The Pageant was originally the creation of a group of Atlantic City businessmen who saw a steep decline in sales after Labor Day. What if the season could be extended for an extra week or two? A promotion to attract the summer renters to stay longer and new visitors to come to Atlantic City for a special event was realized with the inauguration of the Miss America Pageant.

A nationwide organization was created to select a Miss America contestant from each state and a local Board of Directors to manage the annual event. The promotion consisted of a series of nightly elimination contests at the Atlantic City Convention Hall, culminating with the final judging and crowning of "Miss America."

The program began in 1921 and was an immediate success, including national press stories and local newspaper coverage in each contestant's home state. The final night crowning of "Miss America"—with a celebrity host, celebrity judges and professional entertainment—was seen on television by millions of viewers, often the highest viewership of the year.

Question: Could we come up with a similar promotion for our store, Gordon's? After all we were also located in Atlantic City.

Answer: Yes. If we adapted it to a local level, suitable for a children's fashion store. The light bulb flashed—a contest for the title of "Little Miss Atlantic City" was born.

To start the promotion, we met with Lenore Slaughter, the Executive Director of the Miss America Pageant. She was kind enough to give us helpful information, including the format for our judges to follow. She suggested the final competition categories: Beauty, Personality, Poise, and Posture—the same as the guidelines for the Miss America contest.

We ran our first newspaper ad announcing the contest and the number to call for more information. The first day the ad appeared only one person phoned.

It dawned on us that one ad doth not a promotion make. We retrenched and sent a direct mailer to our mailing list with an application, explaining how the contest worked, including the age and resident requirements—girls, 6 years to 12 years of age, who lived in Atlantic County. They had to come to Gordon's with an adult to submit their application.

The mothers of those girls came to our store to pick up applications. By the time of the first week's contest, we had 150 entries—enough for 25 young girls in each of the scheduled six weekly contests.

Next, we contacted local merchants asking them to give us (free) gift certificates as awards to the weekly contest winners in exchange for publicity in all our Little Miss Atlantic City advertising. Those businesses that agreed were also designated as "official locations" (in addition to Gordon's) for parents to pick up applications to enter their daughters in the weekly contests.

> FACT: It is far, far easier to have merchants give merchandise or gift certificates for prizes. It is very difficult to have them give money.

However, we needed to create more excitement for the final contest. We decided the event would be in the evening and the judging would be preceded by a fashion show.

Why not have several of the judges from the children's fashion industry?

Why not contact manufacturers whose clothing we will be showing in the fashion show sponsor scholarships to the winner and runner-up?

But how could we convince them to be sponsors? One way to persuade them is to create a movie! A local cameraman agreed to film a five-minute movie titled "The Little Miss Atlantic City Story," using our store as background and our children as models.

I carried the finished film with a heavy movie camera to the New York offices of our best manufacturers of girls clothing and a promotion package to show them the marketing possibilities. They watched the movie and several of them were impressed enough to give us a few hundred dollars of Government bonds for the winners.

The most interesting event was at a sales convention of children's clothing manufacturers in Atlantic City. My salesman for a prominent girls' dress line made arrangements for me to show the film to his boss at a local hotel. I arrived early with my camera, the movie, a projector, and screen. The owner, his wife, and some friends were there. They all looked a little confused when I announced, "Here I am with the movie." I closed the window drapes, switched off the lights and turned on the movie.

Five minutes later I switched off the movie turned on the lights and opened the window drapes. No reaction. Then, someone in the room asked, "What was that all about?"

My salesman had never told them I was coming. They didn't know me and certainly never heard of Little Miss Atlantic City. When I stutteringly explained what I was doing, the owner laughed and agreed to the scholarship prize. As I left he said, "We were very nervous. We thought someone hired you to show us a pornographic movie."

We eventually had 13 national children's clothing manufacturers and 11 area retailers as sponsors of Little Miss Atlantic City.

The contest consisted of six weekly elimination contests held on Garden Pier in Atlantic City. The girls sat across the stage in chairs. I was the emcee, with my partners handling the contestants, the audience (parents, other family members, and friends of the girls) and the judges. When called, each contestant walked across the stage to where I stood with the microphone. I asked them questions and each girl answered. She would then return to her seat and listen to the next contestant.

One question I always asked was what they wanted to be when they grew up. Some of the answers would have made Art Linkletter proud.

"I want to be a horse when I grow up so I can run through the fields."

"I want to be an IBM operator when I grow up. If machines are going to replace people then I want to be in charge of the machines."

However, America could take comfort that most of the participants gave the traditional answers of young girls: actresses, models, dancers, nurses or mothers.

Women from area civic clubs judged the winner and runner-up. These weekly winners would compete in the final competition to crown Little Miss Atlantic City.

We did have some unexpected problems at the weekly contests. Some of the smiling, friendly faces of mothers who came to cheer for their daughters at the weekly contests became transformed into nasty, vindictive monsters when their daughter did not win. One mother screamed the contest was fixed. And the child that won that week was ugly.

I started to wonder if this was really a good idea.

Talent was never a part of the contest but this did not stop stage mothers coming, unannounced, to our store with their daughter alongside, waiting to perform an impromptu arabesque or break into a song from "The Sound of Music."

These weekly winners would compete in a final competition in a large fashion show at our store wearing outfits from our new clothing lines for fall and winter and receive gift certificates and U.S. bonds. Little Miss Atlantic City, her runner-up and the other weekly contest winners would also ride in their own float sponsored by Gordon's at the Miss America parade on the boardwalk.

After the first year, there was such a demand for seats at the final night, we had to move the competition to a large room at the then elegant Claridge Hotel on the boardwalk. It became a bona fide city event. We charged $4 a ticket to pay for the additional expense of the room and a dessert buffet. About 500 cheering parents, relatives and friends attended.

When the fall fashion show was over, the judges totaled their scores and handed their results to me. The time had come to announce the winner. There was whooping and hollering and screaming as flash bulbs exploded and cameras clicked away and I announced the name of the new Little Miss Atlantic City.

The winner bowed to the audience and slowly walked down the runway with an arm full of roses. The current Miss Atlantic City (who was competing as Miss New Jersey in the Miss America

Pageant) awarded the winner's crown and robe to the happy young girl and I did my Bert Parks imitation of "There She Is..." The next day the local paper gave it front page placement.

The promotion's publicity continued. Within a few years sponsorships grew to include local banks and utilities. Allied Chemical invited the winner to their offices in New York City's Times Square building. She appeared on the front page of Sunday newspaper supplements, led parades and opened new car show rooms.

Then, one day, I wondered what we were actually doing. What began as a way to promote our new fall and winter clothing and enlarge our customer base, had taken on a life of its own. No longer was Gordon's reputation dependent on being the fashion leader of children's clothes in the area but rather the home of Little Miss Atlantic City. We had created a Frankenstein. So, as suddenly as we began, we ended the promotion.

When people came in and asked for applications for the contest, we simply told them, "Little Miss Atlantic City doesn't live here any more."

Chapter Four

A Snapshot of Clients

Food Marketing Institute

Food Marketing Institute, or, as it is commonly called, FMI, is the association for food retailers and wholesalers. FMI is an industry resource on food, advocate for consumers, and host to important industry conventions.

But to me, FMI represents the man who was the president during the prime years, Bob Aders. Bob gave me the opportunity to be FMI's top convention speaker for 20 years. From that platform, I was asked to speak at most state grocery association meetings, wholesaler conferences from the U.S. and around the world, brand manufacturer meetings, as well as consulting assignments with many chains.

Bob and his wife Tabby coincidentally own a home in Atlantic City. Bob happened to walk into Gordon's one lucky day for me. On the wall in our store next to the back entrance was posted pictures of celebrities who visited our stores through the years or whom I met during my presentations...even some letters from well known people like Eleanor Roosevelt, President Ford, and artist Norman Rockwell. Customers enjoyed seeing them and made them feel they had come to an "important" place.

Bob, looking at this memorabilia, asked if I was in the store.

My sister-in-law Shirley called me on the store's intercom to come and meet this interesting stranger. I did. Funny story: during our conversation, we talked about economics and the possibility of New York City going bankrupt. I told him I was dismayed at the New York *Daily News* headline, "Ford Tells New York: Drop Dead." Bob replied, "That's not so. Ford is going to help New York." How did this stranger know? I asked myself. Then I found out Bob had been the Assistant Secretary of Labor serving in President Ford's cabinet and was well connected in Washington, DC.

Also on the photo wall was a large poster, advertising a major seminar I did with speaker partner Ray Considine called, "The Great Brain Robbery." Bob looked at it and asked me "Could this program work for the supermarket industry?" I said (in my naive and positive mode), "It certainly can!"

I learned later Bob was working to consolidate the two existing supermarket trade organizations into one. He succeeded and called the newly merged group, Food Marketing Institute (FMI). Their Board of Directors named him the CEO because of his success in the merger but also because he was the CEO of one of the country's largest supermarket chains.

When Bob was ready to inaugurate FMI's first major supermarket convention, his secretary called me to say, "Mr. Aders asked me to call you and have you create the marketing program you call 'The Great Brain Robbery' and design it for the supermarket industry's first annual convention."

I agreed and asked, "What would be the size of the audience?" She answered, "About 4,000." I was astounded. Four thousand people! I had never spoken to any group that numbered more than a few hundred. But I accepted the challenge.

After inviting Ray Considine to join me in this important assignment, we settled on the title for our program, "Sixty Ideas in Sixty Minutes," and created a presentation of slides, videos, and comments between Ray and myself. Our fast-paced show gave the audience a potpourri of successful marketing ideas and showed them how to adopt the ideas for their supermarkets. The program was a big success. Even though Ray and I lived on opposite ends of the country, we worked together on the show for several years until our differences made it too difficult to continue and we ceased our partnership. I was invited back for every FMI convention to do a major original show for 20 consecutive years!

On my 80th birthday Bob sent me a personal birthday greeting commenting on my annual show for the FMI convention:

Your show was far and away the major attraction to the educational part of the FMI convention.

Your earliest audiences were in the thousands. All of them thought you were a major contributor to their own understanding of how they could improve their own performance.

A whole generation of grocers benefited from your creativity and hard work. I thank you on behalf of all of them for all the good things you did for the supermarket industry.

—Bob Aders

Greenwich Workshop Limited Editions Prints

Ray Considine and I were doing a series of marketing seminars for banks across the country when a member of Iowa Bankers at the state convention approached me for help in his "regular business" which turned out to be an art gallery in his home town.

He was impressed with my ability to take newspaper ads from several audience members, sent to me before the meeting, and give them a twist for a more effective selling message to make marketing points in my presentation. He felt the kind of ideas I gave to banks could work as well for art galleries. Would I mind if he submitted my name to Dave Usher, president of Greenwich Workshop, to be a speaker at their next convention, since they were his main art supplier?

I was delighted to start learning about another industry and how to help the retailers. My answer was "yes." Little did I know then that Ruth and I would be working with Greenwich for more than ten years, visiting galleries all over the U.S., Canada, the U.K., and Australia. After I spoke at that first convention, the audience gave me such high ratings Dave invited me back for the next ten tears to give the galleries more marketing ideas to increase their business.

What made these meetings so interesting was that the artists attended as well as the gallery owners and Greenwich staff. The conventions were usually in Phoenix and we loved going to the Southwest. Ruth's sister Shirley became involved with the work and she and my brother-in-law Milton often came with us.

Greenwich published signed limited edition prints of original paintings. Subject matter was western, Native American, nature, aviation, and fantasy. At the peak of its success, Greenwich added a plethora of subjects to fit all the diverse needs of decorating the growing number of new homes. The galleries that stocked Greenwich art sold the products, not only because of the fine quality of the prints and the beauty of the initial paintings but because of the selling message that Greenwich limited edition prints increased in value for resale.

One of their most profitable artists was Bev Doolittle, known as a "camouflage artist." The distinctive designs and patterns in her paintings led viewers to discover images, which at first viewing were hidden in her work. She said, "I use camouflage to slow down the story telling in a painting but my messages about our wilderness and native peoples are never hidden."

Ruth and I admired Dave Usher for creating an art business that in turn gave many retail galleries quality limited edition prints to sell. In addition, he backed them up with marketing, a vigilant customer service staff, and a great annual convention where retailers could mingle with their favorite artists and preview artwork in progress.

Dave Usher was an avid outdoorsman and nature lover—both a bon vivant and natural leader. At one of our last conferences, he presented me with Greenwich Workshop cuff links and Ruth with a charm for her necklace, which she wears to this day. Sadly, Dave lost his life in a boating accident, but his memory and innovation lives on in his company that still brings to the public the finest in collectible art.

He was a memorable client. *Sic transit gloria.*

IGA

IGA stands for Independent Grocers Alliance. Frank Grimes, a partner at W.W. Thompson, a Chicago accounting firm specializing in serving wholesale grocers, launched IGA in 1926. The face of IGA in my time was Tom Haggai, President and CEO, until his recent retirement from that capacity. Tom is still the international spokesperson for IGA.

I had just finished my annual show at the FMI convention when Tom approached me. He said, "I really liked your show today, Murray. You used one sentence I wrote down because it's a good rule for any business to remember. You said, 'Your customer is not anyone. Your customer is someone.' I would like the several hundred stores in our Alliance to focus on that idea in their marketing."

(That feeling is reflected in their slogan: Hometown Proud—still used today. It emphasizes IGA's contribution to the communities where the owners and staff live and work.)

Tom asked if I would create an annual program for their convention. I agreed. For more than a decade I wrote and presented an exciting original program. We based our show on the five IGA retailers who competed each year for the title of Retailer of the Year. Eventually IGA decided to have annual winners in different departments like perishables, meat, etc.

Because we were independent retailers ourselves, Ruth and I enjoyed working with IGA people. We supported their goal to preserve and grow the businesses of independent grocers. Since IGA's Board of Governors included representatives from all the wholesalers that supplied their products, we became knowledgeable of that part of the Alliance and eventually did many programs for wholesalers.

We developed close association with two of the wholesalers: Wetterau and Copps. In fact, since Wetterau had a very professional event team, we began to use them for all our FMI shows. Ruth and I would travel to Wetterau's office in St. Louis with our slides and videos. Their audio-visual people would put the show together and we would even make a return trip for a rehearsal.

Michael Copps, the CEO of Copps, gave me the occasion to come up with one of my best marketing ideas. Mike asked me to send him a marketing proposal as he was opening retail stores in addition to his wholesaling for IGA grocers. I thought a minute, smiled and said, "The Copps are Coming!" Michael Copps hired me on the spot.

During Tom Haggai's leadership, IGA continued to grow in the U.S. and, with his guidance, IGA expanded internationally— the biggest international growth came in Canada and Australia. I was privileged to do IGA shows in both countries.

One of the most interesting stories in the IGA lore is how Tom became connected to the Alliance. A Baptist minister, Tom Haggai had a radio show. On one broadcast, he had nice words to say about the Christian Science Church. Kay Kyser, leader of the popular Kay Kyser Orchestra, happened to hear the program. He was so impressed that a Baptist minister had something good to say about his church that he wrote to Frank Grimes, a Christian Science friend living in retirement in California. Frank forward to information to his son Donald who had succeeded him at IGA, suggesting that Tom Haggai might make a good speaker at the next Southern IGA Convention. The rest is history...

Even when I was no longer involved with IGA shows, I was able to be of help to Tom Haggai again. Tom had created a foundation (THA) to raise scholarship money for the education of young men and women committed to careers as youth leaders and teachers. He asked me to create a slogan for the foundation, which I did—"The Quiet Trust."

Tom is still a valued friend.

Frank Lalor

I had just finished one of my annual presentations at the Montreux Symposium direct marketing conference, when Frank Lalor came from the audience to greet me. I knew Frank because he was the unofficial representative of direct marketing in Ireland. Frank was well known in Ireland for putting together successful direct marketing programs. He had brought me to Dublin on two occasions for one-hour marketing seminars which he promoted.

"Hi, Murray. I have an idea to share with you. I liked your presentation today and think you should come to Ireland with it but expanded to an ALL DAY show." This was something I had a never done but before I could demur, he went on enthusiastically.

"This is going to be something never done before in Ireland. You will be doing the first all-day marketing, advertising, and promotion program in Ireland, and I know how to make it successful. We will hold the event at the Point Theatre."

The Point Theatre was the largest venue in Dublin and held several thousand people for shows such as the famous Irish dancer troupe and rock stars.

After that, a flurry of letters and phone calls began back and forth between my office in Atlantic City and Frank's in Dublin. I asked Frank for a more detailed explanation of his plans to make the event successful.

"I expect to fill the house," he said to me over the phone. "I'm sending a direct mail package to every small and large business throughout Ireland to promote Murray Raphel, the marketing icon and idea machine, and his day long marketing seminar at the Point.

"When the marketers and business people sign up for your show to hear your great ideas on how to increase their business, they will also receive immediate benefits:

• A free copy of your book, *Mind Your Own Business* (value: $30)

• A savings of $2,000 (equivalent) when a company registers four delegates to the conference

• Special savings from An Post (the Irish Post Office) on their next mailing

• Reduced airfare on Virgin Atlantic London – Ireland (for those attending the conference from the U.K.)

• And more...much more."

I couldn't say "no" to those plans!

I found out later Frank garnered testimonials from people attending my previous seminars in Ireland. An example:

> *I would cross the Atlantic to listen to Murray Raphel. And I have!*
> —Feargal Quinn, managing director, Superquinn Supermarkets and a member of the Irish Senate

Frank even topped all those marketing ideas. Driving down Dublin's main roads, upon our arrival in Ireland, we could see large metal billboards reminding viewers with giant letters about the coming conference, "MURRAY RAPHEL PROFIT CONFERENCE MAY 1," with a giant arrow telling the car driver which direction to go.

Frank did a superb job in marketing. Thousands of businesses signed up ahead of time and hundreds more the day of the conference.

PS: The success of this program and the positive reviews in the Irish media prompted An Post to hire me to do marketing seminars in communities throughout Ireland, encouraging business owners and managers to spend more of their advertising dollars using direct mail. Which leads me to another favorite tenet of mine: "Dollar for dollar nothing succeeds like direct marketing, done properly."

Irish Life Assurance Company

"**A**nd now, let's have a big hand for that international speaker, James Farrell!"

> *On May 25th, Mr. and Mrs. James Farrell checked into the Westbury Hotel in Dublin, Ireland. This was not their real name. They arrived under an alias so no one would know who they were. In the short 72 hours of their stay, "Mr. Farrell" appeared on the stage of the world famous Abbey Theatre and gave a two hour inspirational and motivational program to more than 1,000 people and then, silently left the country...*

Irish Life Assurance PLC promoted for their convention of brokers a "mystery speaker"—an "international marketing expert" as "someone who will show you how to increase your sales." The advance notice was so exciting that I wanted to go to Ireland to hear this amazing person until I realized they were talking about...me.

Irish Life was seeking a tool, a vehicle, a direction these brokers could use to show the clients the new and exciting products Irish Life was about to offer.

What could that new marketing technique be?

Some of the marketing people from the company saw me work in Dublin and concluded they had found the needed tool:

Direct Marketing!

Their first move was to design the mailers themselves. They created letters for their brokers to send to their current and prospective customers. The brokers didn't have to be creative or imaginative. All they had to do was mail the letters.

But they didn't.

They figured, "I've been doing business successfully the same way in the past, so why should I change?"

How could Irish Life change their minds?

That's when they contacted me to be the speaker at their annual convention. I would show the invited brokers (the most successful) how direct mail would put even more dollars in their pockets. But they didn't want the audience to know I was the invited speaker. "Everyone will know who I am," I told the organizers. "I'm well known in Ireland since the promoter Frank Lalor brought me over to speak several times. He blanketed the country with publicity for my last all-day seminar. I'm sure many of your brokers were in the audience for my all-day program."

"They don't know it's you if nobody tells them," they answered.

Don't tell them? That was a novel idea. And one in direct contradiction to everything I knew about promotion. Why have a program unless you create excitement with the speaker?

But since Irish Life was paying all the expenses for the brokers to come to the event, they were assured of a good audience, so no need to argue against Irish Life's speaker of mystery.

We arrived at the airport and were told to wear dark glasses and hats. Ruth wore dark glasses and a scarf—and not to talk to anyone on the plane and not to "mingle" with the crowd when we left the plane to go through customs. An unidentified driver would meet us holding a sign saying, "Mr. and Mrs. Farrell."

Who was that? Someone else on the plane with us? Bodyguards? Other speakers? The name wasn't familiar.

"That's you," we were reminded. "You are arriving incognito. We don't want anyone to know you're in town. It's a surprise.

Don't forget to wear the disguises!"

We arrived in Dublin; appropriately did not mingle, went through customs where we seem to receive ten times more scrutiny than if we had arrived "normally." One young person even approached me, tentatively asking me for an autograph. "You're somebody important, right?" she asked. I mumbled, "Not really," but signed her book "Best wishes, James Farrell."

"It's James Farrell!" she told her mother, all excited.

Then we saw a tall man with a small sign saying, "Mr. and Mrs. Farrell."

"That's us," I told Ruth and went over and introduced myself, "Hello, I'm Mr. James Farrell and this is my wife, Ruth."

"Shhhhhh," he cautioned me, "You need to be discreet." He took me by the elbow and escorted me to a waiting car.

The car was a limousine with tinted windows and had already attracted a small crowd.

"Must be somebody important. The car's got tinted windows." said someone. A woman approached me and said, "Can I have your autograph? Make it out to me daughter Kathleen."

"Certainly," I said, and was about to introduce myself as "Mr. James Farrell, the well known cinema star," but the driver pushed Ruth and me into the car and drove quickly away.

We arrived at the Westbury hotel but not at the front entrance ("Someone might recognize you," explained our driver). Instead we went to the trade entrance under the hotel. There, on schedule, someone was waiting, opened our door, and took us to a secret entrance.

I mumbled to Ruth, "Why didn't they call me James Bond? I'd like that better..." She said, "I can't see anything. The glasses are too dark. Is it nighttime?"

I warned her not to take them off. If she did, she would probably be quickly surrounded with dozens of people saying, "I know you. You're Ruth Raphel from Atlantic City, New Jersey. Why are you wearing that big scarf and dark glasses?"

Inside the secret entrance there was a small elevator that

took us to the hotel's penthouse suite reserved by Irish Life.

We were met by a small select group of senior managers all sworn to secrecy. They called me "Jim" or "Mr. Farrell," asking, "What would Mr. Farrell like to drink?" I restrained myself from answering, "I give up. Why don't you ask him?"

We took off our dark glasses and realized it was daytime. We were asked to go to an adjoining conference room. There we were given ideas and suggestions for marketing their new products and could we please mention them in our talk? We were obliging and said, "Oh sure," and "You bet," and "Of course, of course," at the same time trying to figure out how to change a carefully rehearsed one-hour presentation that was scheduled to start shortly.

While we were listening and nodding and agreeing, the brokers were arriving from all over Ireland at the main headquarters of Irish Life in Dublin. There, they had tea and coffee. (Later we found out that a few asked, "Where are all the big shots? How come they're not here?" No one could tell them they were entertaining that dashing international raconteur, James Farrell, in a nearby hotel.)

After tea and coffee, they were greeted by a key person from the main office and asked to follow him. They left the headquarters building and marched Pied Piper style down the street, about 1,000 brokers following their leader across the main street and through the door of the world famous Abbey Theatre.

The brokers were wondering, "What's going on?" but went into the theatre and sat down. The chief executive was backstage, reminding me of the fifteen or twenty "very important" items to include in my presentation. Suddenly, he shook hands saying, "Best of luck," and walked out on stage.

He welcomed the brokers, said a few words about new products they were introducing, and said, "Today, we're going to show you how to sell those products through direct marketing. And here is our surprise speaker, someone you know and have read about...Murray Raphel."

There was a great burst of applause at the end of my presentation. I even managed to include all the major points senior management had thrown at me. But I couldn't help wondering if there weren't a few disappointed in the audience who were probably saying, "Raphel? Raphel? Hey, I thought we were going to hear Jimmy Farrell!"

Nordic Direct Marketing

This is the story of the day I was a VIP attendee at the Olympics in Norway.

It all began with a phone call from Lars Christensen in Norway. His country was the host that year of the Nordic Direct Marketing Days annual convention. Representatives from Sweden, Norway, Denmark, and Finland would attend this big event and would I come as speaker?

Sure. You bet. Why not. We sent him a proposal.

He called and said because the program was sponsored in part by the governments of these countries, they had a limited budget. Could we adjust our costs?

I looked at the date and said to Ruth, "Hey—this speech is the same time as the Olympics in Lillehammer just north of Oslo. Why don't you make a deal with them saying we'll reduce expenses if they give us two VIP tickets for the Olympics opening day ceremonies?"

Ruth made the offer and they quickly accepted.

Great! We were going to Oslo to give a speech. But, and as important, we were going to the Olympics! As VIPs!

At that time, my nephew Steven had bought a large American flag for our home. I asked him to loan me the flag before we placed it at our entrance. I would bring it to Norway. During opening ceremonies, Ruth and I would stand up and wave the big flag back and forth and everyone at home would see us on TV. The U.S. networks would certainly pick up THAT shot!

We arrived in Oslo and went to the Oslo Plaza, one of the city's finest hotels. Greeting you as you enter is a larger-than-life-size statue of famed skater Sonja Henie. The lobby was filled with CBS TV staff and their cast of hundreds to cover the Olympics. No one recognized that I was a VIP. They would soon know when that American flag began waving from the stands . . .

The next morning Ruth woke up with a severe sore throat. Through the day it became progressively worse with her having trouble swallowing. Upset I called Neil and told her she'd take the next plane home. His question: "Don't they have doctors in Norway?"

That made sense. We checked with the hotel's concierge and he told us to go to the nearby shopping center. Shopping center? Yes. It seems there are clinics in their shopping centers. We went and what seemed to be a teen-age replica of Doogie Howser took care of her saying, "Take these pills. You'll be fine."

We left and Ruth said, "He's too young. These won't work." She said I should cancel her visit to the next day's Olympic events.

I called Lars and he said he was sorry Ruth would not be going but he had a nephew who would be excited to receive this rare ticket.

The next morning, Ruth amazingly recovered!

"I want to go!" she said. But Lars had given away the ticket. I said, "Take mine."

"No," she said, I'm still not 100 percent. You go."

We went back and forth but she insisted. "You go to the ceremonies and I'll stay here in the hotel. They have a large color TV in front of a fireplace with an American announcer and the hotel is providing a smorgasbord. I'll be fine..."

Reluctantly, I left her in front of the television screen and joined Lars and his nephew on the three-hour train ride to Lillehammer. There were buses waiting for us to take us to the stadium...almost. The stadium was a short 10-minute walk. But the farmer who owned the land in front of us didn't want anyone crossing his field. So we walked a zigzag pattern to the distant next field and headed back toward the Olympic stadium.

Picture thousands of people, packed together, walking in a five-foot wide path surrounded by 6-foot high mountains of snow. We moved forward, literally, inch-by-inch. It took us one hour and 45 minutes to come close to the stadium (instead of ten minutes!). And it was COLD!!!

Suddenly, from the distance I heard "Ta-da-da-da!" It was the stadium trumpets announcing the start of opening ceremonies. We were still at least 15 minutes away. "Lars!" I yelled to my trusty leader walking in front of me, "They're starting without us!"

He turned and said, "Don't worry. I have a solution." He reached into his knapsack and pulled out a miniature television set with a three-inch screen for me to watch the ceremonies. So there I was, moving inch-by-inch along the icy path, cold, pushed in all directions by an angry crowd, watching the opening ceremonies on a three-inch fuzzy black and white screen with an announcer speaking in Norwegian.

(In the meantime, Ruth is back in the warm hotel, watching the event on a large color television screen with the announcer speaking in English while she drinks wine and eats Scandinavian delicacies.)

We finally make it into the stadium and discover they sold too many tickets! "Where do we sit?" We asked Lars.

He answered "Oh, didn't I tell you? The only seats are for the VIPs." Isn't that us? I'm a VIP. It says so on my ticket. It seems there are vips and VIPs. I was the former. The latter were the royal family, Olympic committee members and sponsors. They have seats. Everyone else stands.

So much for my VIP card; however, another and much larger problem soon developed. As you walked into the stadium, you were supposed to peel off to the left or right, up or down the aisles. But they were so crowded; the aisles were congested with people. So you couldn't go anywhere except forward!

The crowd in back of us didn't know this, so they kept pushing.

At the end of the path was a metal railing. I could visualize the railing destroyed by the swelling crowds of people and everyone falling 150 feet down onto the ski ramp. Young parents with small children were crying as they held their children above their heads screaming for people to stop pushing.

My immediate reaction: "If I fall, I'll whip out the flag and use it as a parachute. The television cameras will catch me as I plummet through the air. They'll see me back home!"

I yelled to my host, who had his seven-year-old nephew on his shoulders to keep him from being stomped on. "I'm leaving, Lars. Don't worry about me." I turned to go back from whence I had come. Now, picture this: I am going in one direction and thousands of people are coming at me in the other direction!

By now I had learned the techniques of not being thrown underfoot: elbows out, pushing forward (remember now, I'm the only one going out—thousands of other folks are coming IN!).

I finally make it back to the entrance where the Norwegian Army has locked arms, keeping a few thousand more people from coming into the packed stadium. They are outside the main gate, yelling and screaming and waving tickets. I was tempted to offer someone my VIP ticket. Instead, I walked slowly away.

The sun is going down and I don't know where I'm going! The town and train station are somewhere in the distance. But where? Suddenly, passing me, is a man walking on skis. I stop him, saying very slowly: "Do - you - speak - English?"

He answers, "You bet, man. I'm with the security force for the U.S. Olympic team. Did you know they sold too many tickets?" I said I was aware of this and asked if could he help me find my way back to the city. "Sure," he said, "It's on my way. Just follow me."

We chatted as we walk and then he suddenly said, "Well, here's where I take off. My house is this way." "Wait!" I cry out, "Where's the train station?" The sun is setting; the path growing darker. He points in a general direction toward where the town is located and says, "Follow the North Star!" And leaves.

North? Where's North? The North Star isn't out yet; and, if it were, how would I know? My only consolation was that if I froze to death, I had the American flag in my pocket to cover me and provide identification.

I keep walking and then, suddenly, a taxi appears! I arrive at the train station and the next train is leaving in five minutes!

Armed soldiers have set up barricades since all the seats on all the trains are reserved. "Your ticket is five hours from now," says a tall blond guard armed with a sub machine gun.

"But wait," say I. "The train will be empty at this time of the day. The ceremonies have just begun!"

"Why are you leaving?" he asks. And then, "Do you speak Norwegian?"

Suddenly, a workman from the train station walks by. I stop him and place the equivalent of $20 U.S. dollars in his hand and say, "I have to get on that train!"

He nods, understanding, says the appropriate password to the guard, and I bound up the stairs as the train is leaving! The few people on board say, "You're leaving so early?"

I was tempted to pull out my VIP pass so they'd know they were speaking to someone important.

Back at the hotel, I found Ruth in the dining room of the hotel. She has found a dinner companion, an English woman who manages the Avon office in the U.K.

"You're back early!" she says, looking warm and cozy. "Did you have a good time?"

"Let me tell you what happened," I said, sitting in the chair next to her as I reach for food and drink, and recount my always-to-be-remembered three-minute VIP visit to the Olympics...

Chapter Five
Clients Who Became Friends

Tony Ingleton

It's amazing that living half way around the world from me, Tony Ingleton became one of my best clients. What's even more amazing, he became my best friend.

I had just finished a seminar for Eddy Boas's Pan Pacific direct marketing conference in Sydney, Australia when a member of the audience approached me and asked, "When's your birthday?" I told him, "January 25th." He replied, "Unbelievable!"

I said that was an unusual response. He introduced himself as Tony Ingleton and explained he had recently returned from his monthly meeting with Milton Black (an Australian astrologer) who told him he would soon meet someone from America, an Aquarian, who would change his life. Tony said to me, "I guess that's you!"

Later I asked him to tell me his business. He explained it began with his father's restaurant in Melbourne called Pickwick. One day his dad realized there were too many days his restaurant suffered from a malady known in restaurant jargon as "snow blindness," the many white tablecloths atop the unoccupied tables.

His father came up with an idea he felt would result in more business for Pickwick and the other restaurants in his town. He called his plan the 'Dine Around.' It was a money saving plan for customers. When two people came to dine at a participating restaurant, there was no charge for the second entrée. Tony's dad had the theory that the lost revenue would be made up in the appetizers, desserts and beverages. The participating restaurants quickly saw an increase in business.

Tony's dad eventually sold the program to Tony who was convinced the idea of Dine Around would work all over Australia. In order to make it a more salable program for the general public, Tony created an annual $69 membership fee package that gave members savings not only when dining out, but he expanded the program to include discounts for rental cars, movies, hotel accommodations and other entertainment attractions. He knew he had to create an exciting package to get individuals to pay this annual fee.

That's what brought him to the marketing conference. He liked what I had to say and bolstered by the prediction of Milton Black, he asked if I would meet with him about this Dine Around program. I agreed.

Tony brought his first marketing mailing piece in a shoebox to my hotel room and asked, "Why isn't my advertising working?" Before I could answer, he continued, "Look it over and tell me what you think. I'll see you tomorrow."

He arrived early the next morning and asked my opinion. I told him, "You have a great idea and you are going to be very successful despite the fact you're doing everything wrong."

"But I want to do everything right," he said. "Tell me what you think I should be doing and I'll do it."

Ruth and I were leaving for home the next day. There was no time to come up with any new ideas. "That's okay," he said, and quickly put his advertising material back in the shoebox. He gave the box to me and said, "Write me back and tell me what I'm doing wrong, how to fix it, and give me a plan for going forward. Then send me a bill for your work and I'll send you a check and my thanks."

The first change we made was to eliminate the paper coupons businesses had to tear out from a booklet. We instituted a new upscale gold and black plastic card for the payment (similar to a credit card) that could be used again and again, every time the card owner dined at a restaurant in the system. Next we approved his changing the 'Dine Around' name to 'The Presidential Card.' Doesn't everyone like to be treated like a President? That was the beginning of a few decades of a marvelous friendship. Through the years I came up with new headlines for the Presidential Card membership letters that increased memberships including the following:

• The Double Guarantee: "The Presidential Card is the only travel and entertainment card that saves you money every time you use it. GUARANTEED." (PC member can send in a receipt for any disputed charge to receive money back plus the cost of a returned card.)

• Would you buy $900 of services for only $69?

(The $900 figure came from a questionnaire we sent to members asking them how much they saved the previous year by using their Presidential Card.)

Next, we changed the tone of the subscription letter to make it more of a relationship between the reader of the mailing piece and Tony. I asked Tony to send me books on familiar sights and attractions in Australia. That information gave me this opening for a very successful subscription letter:

Growing up in Melbourne, I sat scrunched up to look younger on the Number Six tram from Swanson Street to Glen Iris because, if you were under 12 years old, you could travel for half fare.

Readers said to themselves, "Hey, I remember that!" and continued reading the copy that gave them the sales message of how much they could save as a Presidential Card member (without 'scrunching up').

But even with the success of these new letters, the increased membership was only in the same proportion of those that did

NOT renew their membership. It was a zero sum game. That's when Tony came up with a brilliant idea of Third Party Marketing. He approached Grace Brothers, Australia's largest department store, and offered to print 600,000 Presidential Card brochures for them to include in their monthly mailing to the store's customers with a special offer of a lower membership fee for a Presidential Card. The success of this program led to another idea: offering the Card to Australian organizations as a benefit package to their members. Tony would supply a personalized Presidential Card and directory for each of their members as part of the annual membership fee. The organization would then pay a negotiated amount to the Presidential Card for this added benefit.

Where to start? Tony knew each Australian state has its own post office union. Since he lived in Melbourne, in the state of Victoria, he was familiar with the officers of the Victorian Postal Union and was able to convince them to offer the Presidential Card as an extra membership benefit for each member. He would charge the organization only $10 instead of the regular $69 annual fee. Tony's benefit would be an instant sale and payment for thousands of customers instead of one at a time.

Besides his family, the love of Tony's life is the Walt Disney experience—the movies, stories about Walt and the theme parks, especially Disneyland in California. He belongs to Club 33, a members-only restaurant right in the Anaheim Park. There is an annual fee to belong and, of course, you pay for any meals.

Tony was so excited when he finally received his membership acceptance, he called me from Melbourne to find out where I would be on a certain date. It happened that Ruth and I would be finishing up our big show for FMI in Chicago the day or so before the mentioned date. Tony said if Ruth and I would fly out to LA, he would meet us there (from Australia) to have his first meal at Club 33 with us. And we did!

That's the kind of guy Tony is—impulsive and generous.

In the years since, he has taken many family members to a great vacation in Disneyland and just people he thought needed to experience the fun, including a woman confined to a wheel chair, along with her caregiver and family.

One year after my program at the Pan Pacific Symposium in Sydney, Tony took Ruth and me on an unbelievable vacation to a spot in the Pacific Ocean off the coast of Brisbane, Australia, right in the midst of the Great Barrier Reef called Lizard Island. Now, who else would have me swimming with giant clams?

Then there was the time when I was asked to speak in Singapore for a direct marketing conference arranged by Eddy Boas. When I told Tony we planned to have Shirley and Milt Gordon go with Ruth and me and that we planned a side trip to Hong Kong, he suggested we stay at his favorite hotel there—the Regent. Of course, he booked a room at the Regent and invited us to breakfast on the balcony of his room.

I remember will the times he met us in Montreux, Switzerland and went with us to Finland...

My good friend Tony Ingleton and I still see each other at least once a year and talk every month. We are happy that his new wife Trish has joined in the friendship with Ruth and me.

Eddy Boas

What Walter Schmid did for Direct Marketing in Europe and beyond, Eddy Boas did in the Pacific Rim. He created the premier conference for direct marketing in his hometown of Sydney, Australia. Not only did and he have me as a featured speaker there for ten years, but we became good friends.

I was amazed at Eddie's ability, energy and successes, especially after I learned he and his family were Holocaust survivors.

As a general rule, the family unit remains indissoluble. It does not disintegrate. It remains intact and shines even more brightly in the wretchedness.
—"A Diary from Bergen-Belsen" by Abel J. Herzberg

The Boas family—Eddy, his brother, mother, and father—was one of the few families that was captured, spent time in a German concentration camp (Bergen-Belsen) and came out as a family—rescued at the end of World War II.

The family returned to Holland. A daughter was born. Later Eddy's father died. Mrs. Boas requested and was issued one of the first visas after the war for her and the children to immigrate to Australia.

Eddy told me about me how he got started in business. "I met someone who was selling second hand TV sets. He was making $40.00 a week and said I should be a salesman; so, when I saw a newspaper ad that Olivetti, the Italian typewriter company, was just opening in Australia and needed salesmen, I applied.

"I was hired and quickly learned that selling was a matter of percentages. I realized a salesman has to make lots of calls to get sales in order to make the percentages pay off. I set a goal of six calls a day or 30 calls a week to make my goal of two sales. I succeeded in that goal and went on from there.

"Later, when I married, my wife and I bought round trip tickets for England. But when we stopped off first in Canada, I found a good paying job in Toronto with Addressograph/Multigraph Company. I soon became their number two salesmen in all of Canada.

"We then decided to return to Australia. There I worked as the sales manager of an office equipment company. A few years later, when they went out of business, I told the landlord my problem. He was working for a company called Permail and said, 'You're a good salesman, so why don't you come to work here?' I asked him what the company did. He said, 'We sell direct mail packages.' I didn't know what the words 'direct mail' meant. But I was broke with a mortgage and two young children, so I took the job and quickly learned selling techniques for direct mail—actually good selling rules for any sales person:

• Always tell the truth.
• Sell a quality product.

"There is no sense selling something and two days later the customer calls you complaining about a problem they had with the product you sold them. If you have to spend half your time handling problems you don't have time to sell new customers."

All this time Eddy was experiencing success with direct marketing. He decided Australia needed a seminar along the concept of Montreux so he created the Pan Pacific Symposium as a yearly event in Sydney. From the first session, Eddy had the best speakers from around the world. As he said later to me, "At the moment of commitment, the universe conspires to assist you."

He also said, "To attend the conference in Montreux, I flew 22 hours from Sydney, Australia to Montreux, Switzerland and it was worth every flying mile. I introduced myself to Murray and Ruth and invited them to come to the Pan Pacific Symposium and for Murray to speak there." We accepted his invitation. We returned for the next ten years and I did programs there for him every year. It was the beginning of a lasting friendship.

Eddy also booked me several times in New Zealand, and with other speakers, we did a conference in Singapore. It was our first time in the Far East.

Shirley and Milton Gordon accompanied us on that particular conference. We found it made sense to book an around-the-world trip. That was a brand new experience for the four of us.

Sightseeing in Singapore was fun, especially when we stopped for drinks at the historic Raffles Hotel, one of the most famous hotels in the world. Writers who stayed there in the past included Rudyard Kipling and Noel Coward. Raffles was built in the French Renaissance style. The Japanese occupied the hotel during World War II. After the war, it was completely renovated and restored to its former elegance.

We also took the time to visit Hong Kong. Tony Ingleton (with his then wife Denise) met us there for a three-day stay at the Regent Hotel, facing Hong Kong Harbor. Tony was our travel guide for an unbelievable mini-vacation.

My friendship with Eddy continued through the years by letters and e-mails. One day I received a phone call, "Murray it's Eddy Boas. What are Ruth and you doing next Thursday?" I answered, "Nothing special, Eddy." "Good," he said, "Donna and I are spending a few days in New York City. Can you come meet us there on Thursday?" Of course I said, "Yes!"

We went, had lunch with them and talked and talked, exchanging "remember when" stories. We returned home later in the day feeling content because we had followed Ralph Waldo Emerson's advice to "keep your friendships in repair."

...Especially with old friends.

Walter Schmid

Talk about luck; talk about having the right credentials at the right time—that is my relationship with Walter Schmid and his creation, the Montreux Symposium Direct Marketing Conference. Walter was the worldwide advocate of direct marketing and I was just getting my feet wet in retail direct marketing in a small business in Atlantic City. He plucked me up onto the world stage and gave Ruth and me access to clients and travel all over the world.

Our personal and business friendship lasted until Walter died several years ago. His gregarious personality is still a happy memory. Ruth and I think of him as "Mr. Europe."

Walter Schmid was a list broker in Zurich, Switzerland. He compiled names and addresses of people living in his area and then rented the list to businesses that wanted accurate contact information for sales purposes. Usually, list brokers do not sell their lists; instead, they "rent" them. Through the years Walter and his staff grew the business to include not only all of Switzerland, but other European countries as well.

Reliable compiled lists were at the heart of the burgeoning advertising medium of direct mail. Walter felt direct mail could grow even faster if there was a venue where bright young creative people interested in a future in this field, as well as the established advertising community, could learn about direct marketing, especially direct mail.

Was there any place where both neophytes and professionals could learn more about this advertising technique and how it worked? There was one place: the University of Munich in Germany offered a course called "The Dialogue Method of Written Sales Communication," taught by Professor Siegfried Vogele.

Walter knew that if there were more companies doing direct mail, list brokers—like him—would have big increases. He decided to contact direct marketing associations in different European countries but soon found out almost none existed. It soon became clear to entrepreneur Walter Schmid this was a niche he could fill.

He began the work of putting together a three-day international direct marketing conference in Montreux, Switzerland consisting of seminars, an exhibit hall with booths for sellers of envelopes, paper, systems, marketing material and representatives of post offices around the world, as well as great evening activities.

To insure international attendance, Walter created a board of representative countries. The board members would set the seminar program (under his leadership) and be responsible for attracting creative and marketing people from advertising firms and companies, along with suppliers, to come to Montreux from their respective countries. This insured a base of professional and international attendees.

The seminar part of the conference would include excerpts of the program taught by Professor Vogele in addition to top presentations from the most successful direct marketing campaigns by creative marketers from Europe, North and South America, Asia, and Australia.

Thus was born the annual Montreux Direct Marketing Symposium.

At that time, there was a monthly trade magazine published in the U.S. called *Direct Marketing* that consisted of articles on how small businesses increased their business through direct marketing. Since we used direct mail for our store with consistent success, I sent the magazine's editor two examples of our successful direct mail promotions, informing him that direct mail was the only advertising we did for both these promotions..

He answered quickly, saying he would buy each story for the magazine, and then asked if I would like to write a monthly column for his magazine on retail direct marketing. I quickly said yes. We agreed on the payment and my monthly column ran in his magazine for nearly twenty years! This column identified me as an "expert" in retail direct marketing and resulted in a phone call for me in my office a few months later.

"Hello. Is this Murray Raphel?" I admitted it was indeed me and the voice on the other end continued, "Murray, this is Walter Schmid and I have a question for you. Would you like to be a speaker at our symposium in Montreux, Switzerland next year?" I knew about Walter Schmid from articles in the magazine, but was this really Walter Shmid on the phone, or a friend playing a joke?

It was really Walter. He said he read my column every month and felt he should have a speaker talking about direct marketing for small businesses. Was I interested? I quickly said, "Yes!" and "Thanks for calling me." Starting that day, my wife Ruth worked with me to create a one-hour presentation using slides and statistics that would give the professionals in the audience a retailer's point of view for success in direct marketing. We rehearsed the finished program many times and constantly reviewed it in the weeks before the conference.

We arrived in Montreux and checked into the magnificent Montreux Palace Hotel. From there it was a short walk to the conference hall. Ruth and I sat down for a short time to listen to the speakers, who spoke in German, French, Italian, and many other languages. By the turn of a dial to English on our earphones, we were able to listen to part of a presentation. From the beginning of the Symposium, Walter was smart about hiring the very best interpreters for his conference.

However, when we arrived at the conference hall for a full day of presentations, including my own, I listened more carefully. The first speaker was a German marketing professor who had received awards for his successful direct marketing programs. About ten minutes into his speech, I noticed a swishing sound through the earphones. I turned to Ruth and asked, "What's that sound?" We both looked at the speaker for the source. We saw that he was reading his speech from a prepared text on the podium. As he finished one page, he turned it over to start the next one. The sound of each page turning created the "swishing" sound we heard in our earphones. Three or four other speakers that followed did the same routine: speaker, standing at the podium and reading from papers.

I remarked to Ruth, "I don't like hearing a speech given verbatim from a text. I don't read from a script. I stand up and walk across the stage giving my performance and using slides. But that's not what the speakers do here." Ruth leaned back and said, "Do what you do. That's your style of speaking. It worked for all the other shows you've done. Don't change."

Then it was time for me. The announcer came to the center of the stage, gave me a short introduction ending with, "And here is your next speaker, Murray Raphel!"

I walked nervously onto the stage, adjusted the microphone to my height, picked up my clicker for my slide projector, told an opening humorous story (which I learned from a great speaker was the way to begin), and I was on my way. As I continued I felt my confidence returning. The weeks of rehearsal with Ruth paid off. I finished with a heart-warming story and the audience responded with satisfied applause. There was Ruth backstage, giving me two "thumbs up."

Since the mostly European audience had never seen this type of animated American performance before, I wasn't sure if the Montreux Symposium board members would accept me as a speaker. That is, until after my presentation when a group of people from the audience, including many board members, lined up to talk to me. Each person had a similar greeting. "Hi, Murray. I'm from Oslo. Would you come to Norway and give that presentation?" "Hi, Murray. I'm from Finland. Would you come to Helsinki and give that same program at our next marketing meeting?" "Hi, Murray, I'm from Sweden. Would you come to our next conference in Stockholm and give that same program?"

Within 30 minutes I received 10 offers to speak at a different country's next marketing conference. Was it my unorthodox presentation? Was it the use of humor in my program? Or was it a combination of both? The result of these offers determined that I was about to begin a new career as an international speaker on the value of direct marketing.

But, the most exciting moment came when Walter Schmid approached me later and said, "Good job, Murray. Would you like to come back again next year with a new program?" Of course my answer was a resounding, "YES."

This was the start of ten consecutive years performing at Montreux.

Walter and I became good friends through the years and he made me a member of his board of directors of the symposium. We traveled to many other conferences together, including the Pan Pacific in Australia.

During all those years, Ruth and I traveled more than 100,000 miles a year around the world doing direct marketing seminars, and always returned to Montreux in the spring for the symposium. At the conclusion of each conference, Walter presented the prestigious Montreux Award to a person in direct marketing, a very high honor in the industry. On my ninth year speaking at the symposium, Walter awarded the crystal statue to me with the inscription, "for spreading the word of direct marketing to businesses around the world." It was an emotional moment for me—not only for the honor but receiving it from an old friend.

What made Walter a friend as well as a client came about from the same interests, the respect for each other, and the several after-Montreux excursions we took with him. The most frightening and the most beautiful was the ride through and around the Alps in a small airplane that Walter had arranged for Ruth, me, Ursula (his Girl Friday), and himself. We wove in and out of the most beautiful mountains in the world, but Ruth and I did not really breathe comfortably until we landed.

We made a great car trip with him to the beautiful Lake Constantine in the west of Switzerland, passing through small towns and still quaint villages with buildings decorated to signify particular crafts. Serene countryside was all around us. Another time we went to lunch by train in St. Moritz, passing skiers, practically alongside the tracks. Walter also booked me personally to speak at several direct marketing meetings in Germany and Switzerland.

Walter's success and reputation with the Montreux Symposium was earned year after year by his painstaking effort and fundamental commitment to present the greatest direct marketing seminar in the world, attended by thousands of international professionals. The marketers who attended will never forget the elaborate dinners at a castle outside Montreux that ended each conference. Walter Schmid only knew how to do things first class because he was a first class guy.

Stew Leonard's

One of the most outstanding supermarkets of all the companies we highlighted for our annual show at the Food Marketing Industry (FMI) convention was Stew Leonard's in Norwalk, Connecticut. Starting with the large supermarket Stew

Sr. owned, the business has expanded to four large stores that his son Stew Jr., who is now the CEO, and other family members manage. A large stone stands in front of the store with a carved description of the Stew Leonard philosophy:

Rule 1: The customer is always right!
Rule 2: If the customer is ever wrong, re-read Rule 1.

We first knew about Stew Leonard because his business practices were extolled in many newspaper and magazine stories. He was featured in Tom Peter's best-selling book, *In Search of Excellence*. I read his supermarket consisted of one aisle winding around the store. Through clear windows, customers could see the pasteurization process of the milk. (The Leonards started out in the milk delivery business.) And contrary to many supermarkets, the number of sizes per product was limited to the most popular. The emphasis was on freshness and quality.

These are some of the statistics reported at that time:

• Stew Leonard's has the largest sales per square foot of any retail store in the world.

• More than 200,000 people visit his store each week.

• The quantity of dairy products sold includes ten million quarts of milk, a million pints of cream, a million cartons of yogurt, a million dozen eggs, 10 tons of cottage cheese, and more than 36,000 pounds of butter each year.

Clearly, this was a store to include in my program at the FMI convention.

I called Stew to set up an interview. He was very cordial, even complimentary, telling me he never missed my program at the FMI convention and brought many of his staff to watch and hear me speak. But even though he enjoyed my programs and read my books, he didn't want to do another interview. I felt stymied until I read a story of one of his newest promotions: if customers took pictures of themselves holding a Stew Leonard's shopping bag in front of a well-known landmark either in the U.S. or abroad, he would post the photos on a large bulletin board near the entrance of his store.

That was my moment of inspiration. Since I was speaking at marketing conferences around the world, I bought a dozen plain kraft shopping bags and packed them in my brief case. Ruth took a picture of me holding up a bag in front of Westminster Abbey in London, the Eiffel Tower in Paris, as well as other sights.

I mailed each picture to Stew with this message: "This photo would have been taken with your shopping bag if you let me come and do an interview with you." When I returned home there was a message for me from Stew. "Okay, Murray, you win. Call me to set up an appointment for your interview." I did, and the story was the highlight of my FMI show that year.

...And so began the mutual admiration society between the Raphel and Leonard families.

Feargal Quinn

I heard tales of this great supermarket chain in Ireland, but in order to plan a segment in an FMI show, I needed to see it myself. The opportunity came when I was asked to speak at a Direct Marketing conference in Dublin. Ruth and I used that opportunity to visit Superquinn.

What we saw was one of the best supermarket operations we had ever visited and, best of all, we met the indomitable Feargal Quinn, his wife Denise, some of the children, and key staff.

Besides the attention to fresh products, bright interior, and cleanliness, some of the innovations were:

• One of the first supermarkets to offer prepared food with restaurant quality

• Posted signs showing photos and names of farmers who grew the products, signs showing the time seafood was delivered and bread baked, signs of department managers welcoming customers, etc.

• Free bones for your pet dog and free knife sharpening
• Nine kinds of trolleys (grocery carts) including twin, baby, and toddler
• Tired? There's a place to sit at Superquinn
• Umbrella service on rainy days
• Ireland's first retail loyalty program, and on and on.

That was the first of many visits to Superquinn. We became friendly with the Quinn family and visited them several times in their beautiful home by the Irish Sea. On one occasion in Ireland, we were invited to their house for dinner but we were with Walter Schmid (founder of the Montreux Symposium) and I said we were obligated to spend the evening with our Swiss friend. "Bring him too," said Feargal. Between those two great storytellers who never stopped topping each other, and the assorted family and guests, it was an evening to be remembered.

On another occasion, Shirley and Milton came with Ruth and me for dinner there on Halloween. Beforehand, I arranged to have paper masks made of Feargal's face so when Feargal Quinn opened the door for us, he was greeted by four Feargals.

Gilliane, a daughter of the Quinns, spent a month with us in Atlantic City. During the day she worked at Gordon's. Of all the young people who interned in our store, she was the best. I was ready to put her in charge of the operation, but she returned to Ireland. Ruth and I actually visited her several years later in Paris when she was married and living there.

Then there was daughter Zoe, a college student at Trinity, who met us in Dublin when Ruth and I were there with Neil and Janis, and very young Ben and Adrienne. She was a great tour guide in Dublin. That was the beginning of a special friendship with her as we met her again several times when she worked in New York as a set decorator for commercials.

Neil developed his own connection to Feargal when we received a copy of his book, *Crowning the Customer*. He wanted us to publish it in the U.S. and Neil worked out an agreement with the Irish publisher and Feargal.

We all thought the book to be the best book yet on customer service. And Neil put together a mailing list of U.S. supermarkets and wholesalers and offered the book at a great price by the carton. The results were outstanding. We received orders by phone, fax, and mail (before email). In a short time we sold out of our original printing of 5,000 books.

Every once in a while, the phone rings and a man with a wonderful Irish brogue says, "Hi, Murray."

Jim Cooper and Jack Keith

In 1976, the citizens of New Jersey passed a referendum that allowed casino gambling in Atlantic City. This was the only location in the U.S. except Nevada that allowed legal gambling.

Within a few years there was a major infusion of millions of dollars from the building of new casinos that created thousands of new jobs. The result—an immediate resurrection of Atlantic City's failing economy. The PR Departments were once again able to build campaigns for Atlantic City as an exciting destination for entertainment, conventions, and vacations.

Despite this dramatic recovery of the city, there remained the question of family friendly entertainment that would be responsive to children as well as adults.

In 1974, the mayor of Atlantic City invited a group of local residents to a meeting to discuss creating family attractions in the city. The mayor suggested as a starting point the empty lot located at the end of the Inlet section in an area called Gardner's Basin.

Its history was intriguing. The protective waterways sheltered pirates. And storm-tossed vessels hid there under cover for the Revolutionary War as well as privateers who stashed their captured vessels in the coves. During Prohibition, rum runners dodged the Coast Guard and brought their illegal cargo ashore here.

Landmark restaurants in the Inlet included Hackney's and Captain Starn's. But after World War II, the area spiraled into neglect. Businesses and families left.

After the mayor of Atlantic City realized the need for family entertainment, he invited a group of area residents to form a volunteer committee chaired by James Cooper, a brilliant and successful local attorney to revitalize Gardner's Basin and lead this group as its chairman. I was asked to serve on this committee as vice chairman.

Jim felt confident this committee could revitalize the area. However, he realized all this work would take time, and persuaded the mayor to have the City Council give our committee a long term lease to develop our assignment without political interference—a brilliant move by Cooper.

Among our first decisions was the hiring of Marty Blumberg, my friend and great architect, to design a "footprint" of what the eventual park would look like.

We were fortunate to have Atlantic City agree to help us get started with a $3.5 million bond issue for new docks, bulkheads, and landscaping. Additional funding came from the new Casino Reinvestment Development Authority and the foundation's nonprofit organization. These additional funds created what eventually became the Atlantic City Historic Gardner's Basin.

The centerpoint of the Basin is the Atlantic City Aquarium, a strong attraction for children and their parents, both local and visitors. It also is a teaching tool about our environment.

A major exhibit in the aquarium is a large tank holding 23,000 gallons of water, featuring the fish of the area and, Groman, a 400 pound loggerhead endangered species turtle. Groman is a perennial favorite.

More than 20,000 people visit the aquarium every year to see the exhibits. A major attraction for children is the touch tank, where children can touch varieties of sea life under the supervision of aquarium staff. I like going to the touch tank to watch the happy faces of the children. It makes me feel glad I was part of the committee that fulfilled their assignment.

There are the two people who are most responsible for the success of Gardner's Basin: Jim Cooper and Jack Keith.

Jim Cooper was the original chairman of the project and is still the leading force. He is indefatigable in his dedication to the maintenance and growth of Gardner's Basin, especially the Aquarium. Jim loves sailing the ocean and back bays of Absecon Island and is devoted to Atlantic City, where he also chaired one of the major law firms. Jim is still fighting to grow the Basin and the Aquarium to be Atlantic City's major non-casino attraction. The Gordons and Raphels have been friends and admirers of Jim and his wife Lorraine (recently deceased) for many years.

On a day-to-day basis, Jack Keith is Gardner's Basin. He is the beloved boss of the staff. Also, a true enthusiast for the environment in general and Atlantic City in particular, Jack was the perfect person to head the project. In his younger days he was a deep-water diver. He loves and understands the ocean and local waterways that are the focus of the Aquarium. But what distinguishes Jack is his managerial ability and fostering the feeling of camaraderie and love for the Basin in the staff. He is never too busy to answer a phone call or an email. Jack is a consummate people person and a friend.

Chapter Six
Direct Marketing Friends

Ray Considine

It happened at Boston Direct Marketing Day in 1978. The speakers presented success stories with this new advertising medium of direct marketing, called "below the line" in contrast to general advertising or "above the line." The definition of direct marketing is the method of communicating directly to a person, one to one, instead of throwing a general message out to the public as a whole.

The first speaker was Ray Considine from California. He had created successful direct marketing promotions for banks. His presentation was humorous and exciting, which the audience enjoyed. Next, I was introduced and came to center stage. I told stories of our store's success with direct marketing and how some of the same ideas were convertible to other businesses.

At the end of the day, Ray came to me and said, "You need help with your presentation skills but you have great ideas. Want some advice?" "Sure. Why not? Thank you," I answered.

Ray continued, "I'm quitting my job to be a full time speaker. There are lots of opportunities. Tell me your opening story again. I'll tape record it." He pulled out a small tape recorder from his glove compartment, pushed down the record button and said,

"Okay, tell it to me now." I did.

He listened, memorized the story line, and repeated it back to me (and the tape recorder) with better phrasing, a different emphasis on certain words. His version was much better. Then he said in his super confident manner, "You have great ideas. I know how to sell an audience. We should work together."

Excited by the offer to work with such a smooth presenter, I said that would be fine. Then, Ray threw out at me the life-changing sentence, "Okay, I'll call you when we're doing our first show together."

A few months later he did call and said, "We're doing our first show together. It's for the World Hockey Association."

"Hockey?" I said. "I don't know anything about hockey! I've never even seen a hockey game."

"Great," he said. "I need somebody objective."

It was the first show we did together. I created a cartoon character named "Peter Penguin" and made slides of him showing his ideas to sell more tickets to hockey games. After the program, one of the team owners said to Ray, "That Raphel guy was pretty good. How many hockey games has he seen?" Ray answered, "If I told you, you wouldn't believe me." "Wow," said the owner. "That many!"

What made that owner think I knew the sport very well is that I applied the same work ethic to my new speaking career as I did to all past endeavors. Before I put my presentation together, I called *Sports Illustrated* magazine and asked to speak to the reporter who writes about hockey. I told him my problem and he suggested I come to his office in New York City and he would help me.

A week later I was in his office. After an hour's conversation, with me asking questions and him answering, he gave me three books on hockey. "They're books for your library," he said. "A gift from me. After you read them, you'll be an expert."

I had just learned a valuable lesson. When faced with a problem you don't know how to solve, go to an expert in that business and tell that person these nine magic words: "I have a problem and I need your help." People will be flattered and curious to know the problem and challenged to come up with a solution.

These nine words have worked for me getting more in very diverse ways: getting comfortable seats on an airplane; tickets for a sold-out Broadway show; entree into an office of someone I need to meet. One caveat. When you make your nine-word request, hold still. Don't persist. The silence becomes oppressive. Another rule to remember, "The first person to talk, loses."

The reporter listened to my problem on how to capture the interest of a hockey audience. He asked me what kind of business I was in and then said, "Your business is the same as your audience's business—the selling business. The only difference is you are selling clothes and they are selling tickets."

That advice helped me think about and answer another question after the presentation Ray and I did for the World Hockey Association. One of the team owners challenged me, "You haven't solved my biggest problem." I asked what that was and he said, "How do I sell 5,000 tickets?" I thought a minute about selling in the new medium of direct marketing and I answered, "One at a time."

I explained what that meant. "Think of your customer base as 'someone,' not 'anyone.' What will win over that one person to buy a ticket? It could be a traditional rivalry, mid-game honoring a player, celebrating birthdays of fans, free pucks, or even a surprise concert by a colorful band. Having a happening at each game will intrigue customers to return again and again. What will bring one, will work for the 'many.'"

Ray and I soon began doing programs for bank associations across the country showing them techniques and innovative programs to increase sales of their financial products.

We perfected different programs for different industries that were original and effective. The audiences became more diversified as our reputation spread.

After several shows, audience members were asking for copies of our book.

Books? What books? We didn't have a book.

So we wrote one. Each of us took chapters we were comfortable writing. The theme for the book came from a scene in a popular movie we had both seen, "Butch Cassidy and the Sundance Kid." There is a scene in the movie in which a posse chases two bank robbers. Trying to evade them but never succeeding, Butch Cassidy (Paul Newman) turned to Sundance (Robert Redford) and asked, "How do they do that?"

We wrote our book to show how the outstanding ideas of successful men and women, who are also problem solvers, work for them and will work for you (the reader) as well. "How did they do that?" Our message: "The answers are in this book, titled *The Great Brain Robbery.*"

We sent the book to previous clients as well as media people and were amazed by the initial reaction. A typical response— *"I'm a fanatic on motivational books and I've read them all from Clement Stone to Napoleon Hill and your book is the most terrific motivational book I've ever read!"...Gannett Newspapers*

We reprinted the book a few times and sold several thousand copies.

Finally, like Martin and Lewis, Abbot and Costello, Laurel and Hardy, Ray and I took different directions in our careers with me spending more time writing and giving seminars, and Ray speaking and teaching. We always had different styles of working. Ray was late with any assignment but usually came through brilliantly; I, on the other hand, needed to begin work immediately and finish with time to spare. We both did well in the direction we chose.

W. Somerset Maugham had a good description of what happened when Ray and I broke up our partnership: "It is no good trying to keep up some old friendships. It is painful for both sides. The fact is one grows out of people and the only thing is to face it."

Monty Dare

On a visit to London several years ago, I had the name of a U.K. direct marketer to contact who was a great fan of mine although unknown to me.

I did and that's how I met Robert (Monty) Dare, one of the nicest of all my direct marketing friends.

Keys of Clacton is an English bed and linen center in Essex County, near the English southeastern coast. It's a family business under Monty's capable direction, that sells products by retail and direct mail. They are famous for their eiderdown quilts, hand made since 1946.

But that's not all. Monty has an additional career as a knowledgeable guide to little known but delightful areas around London. He is a student of English history and a source of wonderful stories.

We have had several great London walks with Monty. He was kind enough to extend his tour to Neil and his family and our friend Marty Blumberg's small investment club. One of our London walks included Shirley and Milton and our friends Florence and Irv Whitman, all of whom still remember that special time.

But the very best tour for Ruth and me is when we visited London about five or six years ago with Paula, Caren, and four of our grandchildren: Will, Anna, Sam and Sarah. Besides the amazing visits to St. Paul's Cathedral, the Globe Theatre, the haunts of Will Shakespeare, etc., we celebrated Will's (Crowley, that is) birthday at Murray's favorite London restaurant, La Perla. The evening ended with Monty and his band of followers attending the London production of *Mary Poppins* and a memorable walk back to our hotel with Monty through some of our favorite London streets.

Monty and I still exchange letters and an occasional phone call. He honored me with a beautiful letter on my 80th birthday in which he said, "I've listened to your tapes so often when walking I mouth the words and on occasions can even do the accent but more importantly, I've taken your lessons to heart and there are about thirty people and their families at a small firm on the east coast of England who don't know it but your philosophies have helped pay their mortgages and put petrol in their cars."

Thank you, Monty. We've learned so much from you...

Ken Erdman

I first became friends with Ken Erdman at a direct marketing conference. We were writing monthly columns for two different magazines. I was writing for *Direct Marketing* on this growing medium of one-to-one marketing and Ken was writing for *Counselor* about the importance of using advertising specialties to increase sales. Since Ken was the president of the Three Marketeers, a specialty sales company, he was an expert on the subject.

In the book we wrote together, *The Do-It-Yourself Direct Mail Handbook,* one of the chapters he authored was on the effectiveness of advertising specialties. This is what he wrote. "There is a scene in the musical *Gypsy* when the young Gypsy Rose Lee is instructed by the older and more experienced burlesque professionals, 'If you want to be successful, you got to have a gimmick.'

"The gimmick," wrote Ken, "is what makes your mailer stand out and apart from the competition in the daily mail." Advertising specialties are inexpensive, useful items imprinted with an advertiser's name, logo, or message given out as free gifts to customers or for a promotion. Pens, pencils, key chains, and calendars are just a few specialties in Ken's magic box of promotion materials.

This Gypsy Rose Lee strip tease idea enabled me to recommend Ken for a place at one of the Montreux Symposium conferences. He actually performed a strip tease at the podium, taking off advertising specialty clothing—one at a time—finally winding up with shorts that also had a marketing message. The marketing audience loved his performance.

Back to our book: knowing the importance of a good recommendation, we contacted William F. Bolger, the Postmaster General of the United States for a testimonial. He quickly accepted and wrote an excellent forward, writing, in part, "Direct mail is really advertising's best kept secret. This publication now broadly shares this secret."

Book sales really took off. *The Do-It-Yourself Direct Mail Handbook* filled a special niche. It told small businesses how direct mail could work for them and the proven steps to make it successful.

In addition to his family and business, Ken was devoted to Rotary, whose motto is "Service above self." Ken was part of a Rotary group that raised the funds needed for the distribution of the polio vaccine around the world that helped eliminate the disease.

He was also selected to represent Rotary in the United Nations. The UN has a representative from two international associations: the Red Cross and Rotary International. That was Ken!

When Ken and his wife Sue celebrated their 50th wedding anniversary, they had a party at a restaurant with family and friends. I was asked to say a few words about Ken. I decided my tribute should be about the many people Ken helped through the years and recalled an old Yiddish legend I thought appropriate: "Legend holds that there are on earth thirty-six saints. They are anonymous and unidentifiable as God's agents. Even they do not know their identity. One may be a professional person or a derelict. They are referred to as Lamed-Vav Tzadikim. Rescuing a sick child or solving a difficult problem may reveal his mission. Mission accomplished—the Tzadik vanishes at once. The act of doing a righteous act secretly is a crowning act of obligation. But the secret is no secret to God. He never forgets. Another unknown person immediately replaces the vanished Tzadik; therefore, the earth is never left without thirty-six Tzadikim."

Ken Erdman, who passed away several years ago, was a Tzadik.

John Erickson & Leif Johnson

Montreux was a gathering of people with like interests that blossomed into lasting friendships. But few friendships resulted in Ruth and I being the Matron of Honor and the Best Man in a wedding of two Swedish direct marketing buddies.

It all began with a phone call from John Erickson who lived at the time in Leonia, New Jersey. John was a Lutheran minister and a direct marketer. He did fund-raising for the American Bible Society. Like me, he was an annual speaker at the Montreux Symposium.

John said, "Murray, I just had a phone call from Leif Johanson in Uppsala, Sweden. (Leif was another member of the Band of Brothers who spoke at Montreux. He was a partner in one of Sweden's largest direct marketing agencies.)

I asked, "What's new with Leif?" He answered, "Wait till you hear this one. Leif is getting married to Ingrid (his long time sweetheart). The big news is he wants to be married in New York City. I have a friend who is the Lutheran minister in a New York Church and he's agreed to let us use his church for the ceremony and I'll perform the wedding.

"Here's the reason I called you. Leif wants you to be his best man!" I replied without hesitation that I'd be excited and honored; then he interrupted me saying, "But here's the most exciting part. Ingrid wants Ruth to be her Matron of Honor."

We went to New York for the nuptials. We met everyone at the church the day before the scheduled event for a dress rehearsal. As Ruth and I entered the large impressive stone church, we looked around and I remarked to Ruth, "There must be room here for 6,000 people."

I met John who was waiting for us and I repeated, "There's room here for thousands of people. I thought today was just a rehearsal day. Who else is coming?" "We're all here," said John. "There's you and Ruth; Leif and Ingrid; my wife Nancy and me; and the organ player. That's it."

The rehearsal went fine and so did the next day's wedding. After the ceremony, John had made arrangements for all of us to have lunch at Café des Artistes, a well-known restaurant, just a few blocks from the church.

VINGT ANS APRÉS

John called again, saying it was the 20th anniversary of Leif and Ingrid's wedding. His message: an invitation to Ruth and me to join the Johansons and the Ericksons for a 20th anniversary luncheon at Café des Artistes, the same restaurant where we celebrated the wedding. And, of course, we did!

Tehyi Hsieh, a Chinese philosopher, said it well: "Life is partly what we make it and partly what is made by the friends whom we choose."

...especially if they are old friends.

John Groman

I met John Groman at a Montreux direct marketing conference and decided immediately that he was one of the smartest men and quickest thinkers I ever met.

While still a student at Harvard Business School, John was a co-founder (with three friends) of Epsilon, a data management company that pioneered database and loyalty marketing programs including frequent flyer miles. John was its Executive Vice President and Senior Creative Strategist.

John also had a talent for creating fund raising letters and strategy for non-profit organizations which made him a sought after speaker in the U.S. and around the world, including the Montreux Symposium where we met.

Currently John is CEO (and founder) of three Bella Sante health, wellness and fitness luxury spas in the Boston area.

Several years ago when Epsilon was a part of American Express, John spoke at all-day conferences across the U.S. to small business owners on the value of direct marketing. Since he had other duties as well, the constant traveling became a burden. He contacted me with an offer for me to take on some of those all day sessions.

At first, I balked at the fee but I was smart enough to listen to John's answer to my hesitation: "What do you think your association with American Express will do for your resume?"

And it did great for me! In addition, I gained valuable information from the material sent me. The people I worked with at American Express were the best support in the conference world. I loved the contact with small business people in the audiences and helping them do more business with the proper use of direct marketing.

Added value: Ruth and I traveled around the U.S. and even to the U.K. and Australia for American Express on their dime. We owe it all to John!

Alan Rosenspan

I first met Alan when I was doing a Direct Marketing seminar in South Africa. He recalled that time in a birthday greeting he sent me many years later: "I first heard you speak in Johannesburg back in 1982. I was literally blown away by you, your presentation, your style, your warmth."

Alan and South Africa will be forever linked in Ruth's and my memory of the greatest journey we ever took. To begin with, we were hesitant to accept the invitation from the South Africa's Direct Marketing Association for me to speak at their annual convention. We were civil rights believers and deplored the apartheid system then in place.

We talked to my brother Arnie, a Foreign Service officer at that time, and his then girlfriend (and later wife) Nancy, an attorney at the State Department. The question they asked, "Is the South African government paying any part of your fee or expenses?" When we answered, "No," they told us to go for it. In fact, Nancy gave us some names to contact of people who were fighting apartheid in addition to a contact name for The Black Sash, a local women's group committed to helping the black population.

Because we were not fully committed to the South African trip, Ruth was able to negotiate the best deal we ever made with a client:

• Two first class round-trip fares from New York to South Africa with a stop-off at Rome going and a stop-off at Copenhagen on the return

• On our arrival in Johannesburg, a flight to the Kruger National Wildlife Park and a three-night stay there

The visit is locked in our memory: the sight of the animals, normally seen in a zoo, roaming freely in herds in their natural habitat, is unforgettable; plus enjoying our meals on the central dining room porch with the view of the expansive reserve before us.

But the most enduring memory happened on the second day. Ruth and I and a couple from Australia climbed into a jeep with the driver and an aid, armed with his rifle, and took off to see the animals. The driver talked into and received information from his walkie-talkie for the best animal sightings. Suddenly, we were off to see a lioness and her cubs. After a mile or so, the driver stopped the jeep. There, way too close to us, on an elevated area, was the family we came to see. The driver knew we needed to get out of there fast. He ordered us to remain quiet as he attempted to start the motor and take us to a safer place.

After a few uncomfortable revs of the motor, we finally

moved away. When we stopped, I looked to comfort Ruth. Not next to me, she was under the seat with her legs and feet dangling out.

Our time in Johannesburg was also exciting because we met with an anti-apartheid couple for dinner (and spoke in whispers). Ruth also spent a day with Black Sash ladies and was privileged to watch them in action, counseling a black woman whose husband had been picked up by the police for staying after dark in the city. What impressed Ruth the most was the dignity with which the woman was treated. Tea was served to this woman elegantly as if she was a highly valued client in a commercial office.

I was convinced we would be picked up at the airport on leaving South Africa and, when the authorities found all the anti-apartheid literature on us, we would be sent to jail without a "get-out-of-jail free" card.

Back to Alan Rosenspan:

Alan and his family moved to the U.S. Whatever Alan learned from my presentation, he has created his own niche in direct marketing over the years through his own special talents. He has received more than 100 awards for his creativity and results, including the DMA's Echo award.

He developed the Creative Strategy Course for the Direct Marketing Association and was a marketing instructor and taught classes at Babson College for 11 years. Alan has written more than 100 articles on direct marketing for publications around the world.

Alan's book, *Confessions of a Control Freak* was so well received he was invited to give direct marketing seminars in Iceland, Australia, Belgium, Canada, Slovenia, Finland, France, Holland, Japan, Norway, New Zealand, South Africa, Switzerland, the U.K., and the Ukraine.

We continue to enjoy a professional and personal friendship.

Chapter Seven

Gordon/Raphel Shared Friends

Florence and Irv Whitman

This husband and wife team walked into Gordon's when it was brand new. They were vacationing in Atlantic City, taking advantage of a few days away from their children's clothing store by visiting ours!

Through the years, we expanded our sizes to teens, then men's and women's while the Whitmans kept with children's sizes but added stores. At one time they had three stores in the Washington, DC area.

We had an immediate positive connection. This led to many buying get-togethers in New York, and a buying trip to Italy and Helsinki, Finland. We all had a love for the business and a desire to give the newest and best to our customers.

We shared many amazing trips including London, the South of France and Slovenia.

We also shared family news, weddings, celebrations, and even our problems. Florence Whitman taught us a great deal about healthy eating. Her husband Irv came from a family with heart problems and she decided early on to keep him alive and kicking. All this was done with a great deal of humor. I think she even knew that Irv cheated on his pristine menu a little, especially when they were at our house where he was exposed to the after-dinner desserts.

Carole and Marty Blumberg

I mentioned Marty previously and the great help he was in giving his architectural know-how to make Gordon's a distinctive place to shop.

In addition, Marty and his wife Carole, were our friends. Carole is deceased but for many years we were buddies and traveling companions. One memorable trip outside of Cannes, France we took the wrong turn off a highway and drove down a mountain road without lights. All except Marty, the driver, knew the danger we were in. We all had our peculiar ways to deal with it: clutching the seat, biting nails, silent praying. Of course, when we finally came to the road at the bottom of the mountain, we laughed it off. Some joke!

Carole had her own successful real estate business. One of her last wonderful accomplishments for the Gordon-Raphel family was the apartment she found for our nephew Steven Gordon in which he still lives in and loves.

Marty is still our partner in the building behind our original store known as The Garage at Gordon's Alley—a former bank garage which now houses Marty's office, Special Improvement District (former offices of Raphel Marketing) and the Greater Atlantic City Chamber of Commerce.

Chuck and Mary Wilson

Dr. Wilson—Chuck—was the prominent black physician in town. I met him as we were both Republicans and interested in Atlantic City and Atlantic County politics. Not only was he an exceptional person but so, too, his wife Mary. She was a fitting partner—smart, capable and fun to be with. We characterized her as "Mother Earth" because she was such a strong family person. We also had children of similar ages and the same outlook on life and sense of humor. There was always a lot of laughter when we were together.

Chuck had an interesting work beginning. After graduating Hampton College, he, with a few other black young men, were hired by the Pepsi-Cola Company as sales people to canvass in the South for sales. They were very successful. It was an important beginning for corporations to recognize the underused potential of black college graduates in the business world.

But medicine called. Chuck and Mary took off as newlyweds to live in Geneva, Switzerland where Chuck studied and earned his degree in medicine. Their first child (and older son Chuck) was born there.

After completing his residency in the U.S., the Wilsons settled in Atlantic City. Although a busy doctor, Chuck was called on for many additional responsibilities. One was an appointment by President Reagan to serve on a task force to combat illegal drugs.

Dr. Wilson (deceased) had the best personality of anyone I have ever known. He was erudite, funny, and kind, and a great storyteller. His patients loved him. When my father-in-law Herman Dichter became ill with a fatal aneurysm, Chuck came to the house and decided he needed hospitalization. Knowing Herman's usual dignity, Chuck drove him to the hospital rather than subject him to a commercial ambulance.

Chuck and I served together on Atlantic County Board of Freeholders. When our son Neil graduated law school, we hired him as our aid. It was a great fit!

The Wilson children did not follow their Dad into medicine, but he was very proud of their choice of careers: Chuck Jr. and daughter Medina became educators and son Jeff, an attorney.

Marion and Jacques Kukurudz

Jacques Kukurudz was the "pop-up king of direct marketers" in Paris. His wife, Marion, was the concierge for the classical concert artists at the Intercontinental Hotel in Paris. They had three sons and an apartment in the city. Nice life!

We met through the mail. Jacques was interested in my direct marketing ideas and we corresponded, finally meeting on a side trip to Paris after Ruth and I were at a Montreux Symposium conference. Later, I was able to have Walter Schmid invite Jacques to speak at Montreux.

There were more trips to Paris and dinners at the Kukurudz apartment. On one occasion, Shirley and Milton and Tony Ingleton (and his then wife Denise) joined us. We had a wonderful dinner together and laughed more than I ever remember. It was that kind of special evening!

Jacques was then invited by Eddy Boas to speak at the Pan Pacific Direct Marketing Conference in Sydney, Australia. I was speaking there also, so again, we had a terrific time with the Kukurudzes.

At about that time, Jacques and Marion were become discouraged living in Paris. There were demonstrations against Jewish citizens and even attacks on synagogues. Although Marion was born and raised in England, Jacques was from France. When the Nazis' power extended to France, Jacques's family sent him with a group of people fleeing France by crossing the Alps to Switzerland.

He was given a home there during the war with a Catholic family with whom he bonded. There was mutual love and he considered them as second parents.

When the disturbances in Paris continued, Marion and Jacques decided to immigrate to the U.S. with their youngest son, Alexander. The two boys, Jonathan and Rodrique, were old enough to take over the pop-up business and decided to stay in Paris.

On the way to their new residence in Los Angeles, they spent time with us in Atlantic City. Once established in LA, Jacques started a printing business and Marion transferred her talent for handling big name classical music artists to hotels in the LA area. Marion, Jacques, and Alexander finally had their green cards and relaxed in their new home. Alexander went on to college, a job as a banker and a family man on his own.

Ruth and I visited them often in LA on our way back from Pan Pacific conferences.

Meanwhile, Jonathan and Rodrique decided to leave Paris. Jonathan left for LA with a wife and three children; while Rodrique, a divorced father with a daughter, remarried and with another daughter decided to immigrate to Florida.

Jonathan's family had particular problems with visas (except for their last child, who was born in the U.S., to the point where Jonathan left the U.S. for Israel. Sylvie, his wife, and their four children now live with Jacques and Marion, keeping their place in the U.S. with education visas.

Jacques and Marion, as head of the family, do it all with love, grace and humor.

Chapter Eight
Family

Ruth and Me

Foremost in my adult life has been my wife and partner, Ruth. We have shared 60 years of a remarkable marriage that strengthens with each year to the point where we can finish each other's sentences, spoken or written. We are as one.

After our initial meeting in Troy, Ruth and I kept in touch the next four years, on and off dating. I finished Syracuse and started working at Miles Shoes in Albany. Ruth went a year to college and then worked as an executive assistant to the manager of the local Swift & Company. (When our three children were in college, Ruth enrolled in Stockton College and earned her BA in Literature.)

The car ride to Atlantic City with no Garden State Parkway was long. One weekend I came down with an engagement ring and three months later we were married in Dichter's Hotel. My parents catered the wedding. Shirley, who was already married to Milton, was matron of honor. We honeymooned by driving to Miami Beach and staying in my Great Aunt's apartment. Those were frugal days!

My in-laws, Jean and Herman Dichter, welcomed me into the family. In fact, we lived at the hotel for a while when we first moved to Atlantic City. Herman loved to fix up his hotel each winter and had a few older, capable mechanic friends who were very loyal to him and became indispensable to us when we built our store.

Our children--Neil, Paula and Caren-- are each different and each one of them is special to Ruth and me. The way we write or email them or write about them is hierarchical by age: Neil, the oldest, is first; Paula, the middle child, is next: and Caren, our youngest, completes the list. We had the unbelievable good fortune (actually, it was our children's good taste) to have them marry the best possible mates—Janis, Jack and John.

The three families: Raye-Raphels; Crowleys; and Franzinis gave us a bevy of wonderful grandchildren: Ben and Adrienne Raphel; David, Caroline, and Will Crowley; and Anna, Sam, and Sarah Franzini. We are proud of them and love them for being loving and respectful to their parents and to us, for being the best they can be, and for being good to one another and others.

The Raye-Raphel Family

Neil

After being a lusty, crying baby, Neil was a pleasant, active toddler. Our baby sitter "Mommy Ida" informed us the crying would stop when Neil could walk and talk. She was right—which proves you should always listen to Mommy Ida. Neil loved his sisters. When he was in kindergarten and Paula, still a baby, Neil was asked by the teacher to name something soft. As his teacher told us, he said, "My sister Paula."

In third grade, the teacher complained about Neil leaving his seat and roaming. Ruth and I came to the class for a conference. Fortunately, a very bright principal, Joe Zavaglia, was there with us. His opinion was that Neil was bored and offered to supply extra work. He looked after Neil until he finished sixth grade and we never heard another complaint from school.

My great amazement was that Neil could lay on the floor,

playing a game while doing homework with the television blasting basketball. Neil was on the high school track team. What we didn't like was watching the runners at the end of a track meet gasping for breath...so Ruth and I cheered his victories but were not there to see him cross the finish line.

Neil graduated high school with honors and was accepted at Swarthmore College. It was a great school for Neil. He did the usual junior semester abroad in Avignon, France and a back packing trip to Europe with friends. After graduation, he came back home and worked for a year as a reporter for the *Atlantic City Press*. Then he went off to the University of Texas Law School, came home again, passed the bar, and clerked for a New Jersey Appellate Court judge.

He tried politics (after working as an aide to me and my friend Chuck Wilson when we were Atlantic County Freeholders) by campaigning for a spot on the Atlantic City Council. He didn't make it. But as he so humorously said, "If I had been elected, I would have asked for a recount."

Then came love and marriage to Janis Raye, a Brigantine resident with whom Ruth arranged a first date. She was one of three pretty sisters who were customers of Gordon's. Before Neil fell in love with Janis, he fell in love with Billie's (future mother-in-law) cooking and Irv's (future father-in-law) card playing. Marriage to Janis was a natural.

Neil and Janis Raye

They moved to New York where Neil worked for the financier Victor Niederhoffer and Janis attended Columbia University Business School. After graduation, Janis accepted an offer to work for Wall Street investment bank Goldman Sachs. They sent her to Tokyo, Japan to open a human services department. On her return to the U.S., pregnant with Ben, she decided to leave Goldman Sachs. Neil left his job and they moved to Brigantine.

Neil decided to be an entrepreneur. He joined us at Raphel Marketing after immersing himself in direct marketing books and techniques. He became skilled enough to be a practitioner and was asked to teach a marketing course at Stockton College. Then Neil established his own niche by adding a publishing division to Raphel Marketing. He was also invaluable to us when we decided to retire from Gordon's by handling the problems of selling our real estate.

Then another business came about for Raphel Marketing— Supermarket College. Neil and I developed the program, obtained sponsors and chose the speakers. Ruth and Shirley took care of the office work and hotel arrangements. We had seven successful years, holding the event either in Atlantic City or Las Vegas. Janis was outstanding as the host who welcomed the audience and introduced each speaker.

Meanwhile, after the Raye-Raphels had their baby daughter Adrienne, they made a temporary move to Haddonfield, New Jersey. Five years later they made another move, settling in St. Johnsbury, Vermont, after finding out about a terrific public/ private high school, St. Johnsbury Academy. They live there in a great home on a hill. Janis joined Neil in business and together they took Raphel Marketing to a new level by promoting giant postcard mailings to supermarkets and offering services in all the facets of internet and email marketing, web design, consulting and extending the publishing recently to a new imprint, Brigantine Media.

The Raphel Children
Our Grandchildren

Ben graduated Swarthmore College and is now working for a Washington, DC international law firm, Crowell & Moring— living with several pals and enjoying the social life of DC. After earning her undergraduate degree from Princeton University, Adrienne is working toward a Master's of Fine Arts from the Iowa Writer's Workshop program of the University of Iowa. She is our poet and writer.

The Raye-Raphels enjoy their time together, traveling or at home, playing all kinds of games, and still competing with one another to win. But they're always open for family and friends to join them.

The Crowleys

Paula

Neil was right. She was soft. We were lucky with her elementary school as she had a marvelous teacher, Miss Bew, who, in an experimental program, stayed with the class through third grade. In grade school and junior high, Janie Packer was her best friend. Every Sunday afternoon Paula organized a dance recital in our apartment over the store. The corps consisted of Paula, head honcho; Janie; little sister Caren; and Caren's friend Lisa Faber. The girls dressed in basic Danskins but added all sorts of props for each number. The audience included the Fabers, the Gordons, and us, and we applauded loudly while Neil and his cousin Norman, convulsed in laughter, acted out their own version of the routines.

High school meant work, but clothes and sorority became important. Paula's mother was against wearing jeans to school even though it was the way to go for most kids. Paula didn't object but later we found she changed to the jeans tucked in her locker at school. Why fight?

Paula was a top student like her brother. Her graduation speech was an essay she wrote titled "The City," which came as a wonderful surprise to us as we believed in the importance of cities, but didn't realize we had passed on the emotion to the next generation.

Middlebury College in Vermont was the perfect place for Paula to study, grow, and develop a cadre of friends. She spent her junior semester abroad in a Beaver College program, living close to Harrod's. What fun! Two European trips with friends: with

Middlebury friend Joan, she backpacked to Italy, Austria, and Yugoslavia. And with friend Bonnie from the Beaver program, a week's horse-drawn caravan journey in Ireland.

After college, Paula and friend Andy Kaplan went to New York City to live. Ab Rosenberg gave Paula a job at his Capezio store while she decided on a career. She landed an executive training job with Saks Fifth Avenue, finished the course, and was posted to the children's department. We were delighted: Saks, one of the top retailers in the country. What an opportunity!

But Paula had other plans. She enrolled for a graduate program in City Planning at the University of Pennsylvania. After receiving her degree, she went on to the Wharton School of Business, for a second master's degree. While at Wharton, her class had a visiting teacher from the Rouse Company, a prime developer of retail city projects, especially waterfront development. He presented a real problem to the class for an opinion how to solve it. Paula's solution was so on target that she was presented with a job opportunity on graduation.

Paula started her career with Rouse on the Gallery project in downtown Philadelphia. On Market East, the Rouse Company was building a city mall connecting two department stores and adding many new retail stores and eating-places.

Her final project with Rouse was opening their major waterfront development called Bayside in downtown Miami. Jack Crowley came along and brought love and marriage. Everything changed.

Paula and Jack Crowley

Paula returned to her apartment in Philadelphia to plan for a wedding and a new job with Linpro Development Company

Jack, a graduate of Notre Dame, not only had a successful business as a distributor for high end medical equipment, but was also a residential real estate entrepreneur. One of the houses he had purchased is where he and Paula started married life.

In the meantime, Paula left Linpro and reconnected with Lou

Sachs, a former associate from the Rouse Company. They formed a company to buy, renovate, and manage community shopping centers. The business carried on until a complete slowdown in that market. Luckily, Paula and Lou saw an opportunity in the healthcare arena. They provided the needed expertise to develop a new type of outpatient facility, based on the principles of retail development, and formed a new company, Anchor Health Properties. Their company builds state-of-the-art ambulatory centers, medical office buildings, and replacement hospitals.

Ruth and I visited the Doylestown Health and Wellness Center developed by Anchor and were overwhelmed by the healing gardens, attention to detail, customer friendly areas, and the great design of the place, so important for keeping up the spirit of patients needing medical attention and their families.

Meanwhile, Jack's business continued to grow with a primary emphasis on the distribution of medical equipment for respiratory patients in hospitals and sub-acute facilities.

Paula, Jack, and their children now live in a beautiful older home in St. Davids, Pennsylvania. They will soon have a vacation home in Beaufort, South Carolina where all their family and friends can visit.

The Crowley Children
Our grandchildren

David, the older of the two boys, graduated from the University of Notre Dame and now works for a wealth management firm in Philadelphia, spending lots of time in New York City with his girlfriend Paula Alfonso who is studying at Columbia University for her graduate degree in International and Public Affairs. Caroline is at the University of Tampa and is majoring in sociology. Meanwhile she is living in her own apartment with a roommate and loving being in charge of her own place... including painting rooms with Dad's help. Will has followed his father and brother to Notre Dame, but is finding for himself the courses and career direction that's right for him.

The Crowley men have a special connection with Notre Dame and golf but all of the Crowleys are involved with helping people and families less fortunate. They also love to vacation together and it looks like there will be lots of togetherness in Beaufort.

The Franzinis

Caren

How do you follow a brother and sister who were honor graduates from high school? If you are Caren, you become one too! Her graduation speech was on Historic Gardner's Basin—very dear to my heart.

We first realized she was not going to be left out when she was five. We had just finished dinner at a favorite restaurant. When the waiter handed me the check, Caren turned to him and said, "My compliments to the chef." Then there was her time in junior high school. As a minority white student, she was elected class president. Her ability to fit in and be responsive to everyone is a signature characteristic.

She started her college years at Georgetown and transferred to the University of Pennsylvania to be an Urban Studies major. She spent her junior semester abroad with the Beaver Program in London. And she did the usual backpacking European travel with friends. One interesting stop was in Geneva, Switzerland to visit Aunt Ruth and Uncle David—the day before their daughter Alexandra was born. Ruth made a sumptuous dinner that probably started her labor pains.

Caren returned to Penn to complete her Master's in Business at the Wharton School. After a stint at a public development project in Philadelphia, she went to New York to work for the Port Authority. Then came an offer to work for New Jersey's Treasurer in Trenton and her meeting with John Franzini.
Love and marriage came next.

Caren and John Franzini

John already lived near Trenton in Lambertville, a small town on the Delaware known for art galleries, antiques, and restaurants. After their marriage, they decided to buy a house right in town. Because Lambertville is such an ideal place to be, they live there today despite replacing and repairing after three floods.

John is an attorney, with a law degree from Rutgers University. He is active in the community and the schools his children attend. He is an outdoor enthusiast, especially bicycling, and rides a bike race each year to raise money for the Multiple Sclerosis Foundation. He is a volunteer coach who gives the players not only points in sports, but more importantly, in sportsmanship. His kids know him as a strict coach who expects them always to play hard and do what is right; at the same time, he is an affectionate and loving father.

After being an assistant treasurer for New Jersey, Caren was appointed executive director of the New Jersey Economic Development Authority. She is still in that position today, having served with seven governors in both Republican and Democratic administrations. She has earned the reputation of supporting projects that have merit and not political expediency.

Caren has been honored innumerable times for her work at EDA for bringing businesses and jobs to New Jersey. One such dinner and honor was given by the Wharton Club of New York. Paula, Ruth and I came to cheer.

Another time, the Raphel and Gordon families attended a dinner to celebrate a project for handicapped people. Caren was a speaker on behalf of the support given the project by EDA. She gave special remarks about Steve Gordon and his success working many years in the casino industry and living independently. Steve received the applause of a hero that night after her talk.

Caren receives thank you emails and cards from employees of EDA because of her fairness and openness with staff, always encouraging them to take responsibility in their jobs.

The Franzini Children
Our Grandchildren

Anna, the older daughter, is attending University of Pittsburgh. Like her mom and Aunt Paula, she is in the Urban Studies Program. She also likes to travel, having recently spent ten days in Israel under the auspices of Hillel in the Birthright Program. She expects to study in Spain for her junior semester abroad. Anna is her Mom's right hand person. As the oldest child, she is there for her brother and sister, especially so during the period of Caren's recovery from breast cancer. Anna also has a close relationship with first cousin Caroline.

Sam is still in high school, very popular because of his friendliness and concern for others. He is a good student and an outstanding athlete who excels in football, basketball, and baseball. One example of his generosity of spirit is when he asked a coach at a basketball game to let him (Sam) sit on the bench so that a teammate, who had not been in the game, could play. The coach was amazed and told Caren and John.

Anna and Sam work full time in the summer and reduced hours in the winter to pay for extra trips and activities. If you need a good waitress or busboy, call them.

Then there's Sarah, a clone of her mother, who takes on responsibility willingly and gladly. When we made the family trip to London a few years ago, she was about seven years old, but had more energy and drive to see and do everything than the rest of us. Knowing her bat mitzvah was approaching, I told Sarah that instead of the honor of saying a passage from the Bible, I would rather read the letter I wrote to her at when she was born. "That's fine, Grandpop," she said. I replied, "The problem is I'm worried that I will be too emotional." "Don't worry, Grandpop," she answered, "You are a professional."

When I watched at the airport, on the return from our London trip, the tableau of the traveling Franzinis being reunited with their husband and dad, it was a picture of a loving family.

The Gordons

Ruth and I shared a business—Gordon's Alley—with my sister-in-law and brother-in-law Shirley and Milton Gordon, and we still share a home with them.

We started out together in the three-room apartment in back of the store and now we live together in a beautiful, Sanford White-designed house, one house away from the Boardwalk and the Atlantic Ocean. We have always have dinner together, and Sunday morning family breakfast is a tradition.

The Gordons have three sons. Steven, Norman and Jeffrey are more like additional children to us than nephews. And the same goes for the Raphel kids, Neil, Paula and Caren, to the Gordons.

In fact, Caren came home from first grade and announced at dinner that she felt sorry for the other children in her class because they only had one mother and one father. She took for granted that she had two of each.

Much could be said how Steven, who has special needs, gave us the purpose to make more money by growing Gordon's Children Store into Gordon's Alley. That's true, and Steven was able to live in a superior residential school until he was educated enough to come back home to his own apartment and a job at Bally's Casino.

But the problems and successes of the store propelled us together as well. We never stopped thinking of ways to increase business or how to do better promotions or find exclusive merchandise. Ask any of our children about the many dinnertime conversations of how best to run our parking lot. They will say in unison, "Ugh!" Or the nights we spent in the store, opening boxes, tagging and straightening for the next day.

We allowed each other's children to work in the store. Steve never missed opening the doors for our big New Year's Day sales and walking the policeman to the bank with the day's deposit. Norman stayed the longest; first as a salesman in the men's store even though his Uncle Murray was a tough taskmaster. But then he opened the successful Alley Deli and was on his own. Jeff opened a young man's store and stayed with it until we retired Gordon's.

Neil never caught the retail bug but Paula and Caren were back-to-school and Christmas season salesgirls until they left for college.

Our families had several fun vacations together when the children were small including one to New Orleans; another to Hersey, Pennsylvania; and a patriotic tour of Jamestown, Thomas Jefferson's home, Monticello, and Colonial Williamsburg.

We were grateful to the Gordons for looking out for our children and my parents, Sara and Harry, when Ruth began going with me to speaking destinations. By that time, she had learned how to process slides and put my shows together. Later, when our children were older, Shirley and Milt were able to go with us on several of the European trips, especially where they could buy for our store.

But what really showed family spirit is when the Atlantic City television station Ruth and I had invested in flopped. The Gordons stood right by us until we worked out of our financial difficulties.

Even now our two families and extended families join for weddings, bar and bat mitzvahs, and, of course, Thanksgiving and Christmas. We are very fortunate that Norman married Jeanne and Jeff married Heidi. Both girls fit in with our daughters and daughter-in-law and they enjoying meeting at our house and at celebrations. Norman and Jeannie's two children, Daniel and Molly, are in college. Jeff and Heidi's children are Jacob and Hailey. Jacob is in high school and Hailey is in middle school.

The Dichters

We are very fortunate to have family who live close to us— Ruth and Shirley's younger brother David and his wife Ruth. They are not only our weekly dinner companions, but they share all special occasions with us and are there for us if we need them.

Besides, we have a special relationship to their children— Alex (Alexandra, sometimes affectionately called "Puggy") and Daniel, better known as "Ollie" to all of us. Before we or the Gordons had grandchildren, they were "it."

David lived overseas for a number of years, including a tour with the Marines and also as a Foreign Service officer in Thailand and Burma. He also pursued a graduate studies program in the Northwest Frontier Region of Pakistan for Birkbeck College, London University.

On his return from abroad, David was a staffer for the Peace Corps in Washington, DC where he met his wife Ruth, who was working for an international development organization.

They eventually settled in Geneva, Switzerland, where Alex and Ollie grew up. We visited them almost every year and the Dichters made return visits each summer.

About eight years ago, David and Ruth left Switzerland to live in the U.S. They settled in a house in Linwood, a few miles inland from Atlantic City.

Ruth joined a French speaking social club who meet weekly for brunch. Ruth is a talented linguist who can easily go from her native Swiss German to French or English. She is a wonderful person who has enriched our lives. Ruth and Shirley do not consider her a sister-in-law but a sister.

Their son Ollie has remained in Geneva as a banking professional with the Swiss branch of the American Bank, JPMorgan. He keeps very connected to the family with emails and visits. Alex received her master's degree in environmental studies from Clark University in Worcester, Massachusetts and works for the EPA in Boston. She is married to Keith Wales, a sociologist. They have a young baby Max (Maximilian) who makes everyone smile, including, of course, the grandparents... and the aunts and uncles.

Arnie and Nancy

Arnie

My brother Arnold Raphel was meant to serve in the State Department. As an elementary school student, he went to the library each month to read the new issue of National Geographic, eagerly looking at the photos of far away places and studying the descriptions. When he learned that Foreign Service officers traveled to all those places, paid for by the government, he wrote John Foster Dulles, then the Secretary of State, to apply. Mr. Dulles advised Arnie to first graduate high school and then attend a college that would prepare him for government service.

Arnie followed his advice. He finished high school, graduated from Hamilton College, and then received his master's degree from the Maxwell School of Citizenship and Public Affairs at Syracuse University. Arnie began his distinguished career at the U.S. State Department in 1966.

During his school years, he met and married Myrna Peretz and had a daughter, Stephanie. Later Arnie and Myrna divorced. Both parents remained devoted to their daughter. Myrna later remarried. She and her husband Carl had a son, Baruch. Myrna is an accomplished pianist and teaches English as a Second Language.

As a Foreign Service officer, Arnie was assigned to the Middle East, mostly in Pakistan, and rose in leadership to become the 18th U.S. Ambassador to Pakistan after his nomination by President Reagan. He spoke both Urdu and Farsi for easy access to the people he met in the region and to his diplomatic counterparts. He loved representing the interests of United States, strengthening the ties between the US and Pakistan...and traveling. And he did it all with intelligence, love for his country, and respect for the people and culture of Pakistan.

In between those missions, he served as executive assistant to several Secretaries of State, including Henry Kissinger, Cyrus

Vance, Edmund Muskie, and George Schultz. He made his mark in that position by championing and bringing diversity to the State Department with more women and people of color. He taught classes to recruits, using humor and a roll-up-the-sleeves attitude and less formality to get the job done.

After a few years, Arnie met and fell in love with Nancy Halliday Ely. They were exceptionally well suited for one another. And when they visited the family a few times, we fell in love with her, too. All of the family joined her at the swearing in ceremony of Arnie as Ambassador. It was a great joy for my parents to be there and meet the President of the United States.

Nancy and Arnie were married at our house after the Senate confirmed his nomination as Ambassador to Pakistan. It was a great wedding. We met Nancy's two sons by a previous marriage, John and Bob Ely. Janis sang a traditional wedding song. The newlyweds left soon afterwards for their new home in Islamabad, Pakistan.

The next year and a half were idyllic, as Arnie not only represented the U.S. in the best possible manner, but he and Nancy visited every section of Pakistan, greeting leaders, business people, and citizens wherever they went, becoming more and more knowledgeable.

Nancy took on assignments with A.I.D. and also spoke to Pakistan women's groups on feminist issues. Their residence in Islamabad became a popular destination for visiting U.S. officials, celebrities and family...including Stephanie.

Ruth and I planned our trip to Pakistan for September after they completed a visit home in August. Arnie's last letter to me, reminded me he and Nancy were looking forward to Sunday morning breakfast at our house with bagels, cream cheese, and lox along with bacon and eggs.

On August 17th, 1988, just before Arnie and Nancy's trip to the U.S., Arnie was killed in an airplane explosion, along with President Zia of Pakistan, U.S. Brig. General Herbert Wassom, and others. Nancy came home devastated. The funeral and burial were in Arlington National Cemetery. All of Arnie's family, friends, and associates were there to honor him.

Columnists and pundits from every major U.S. paper and news magazine paid tribute to the service Arnold Raphel gave to the State Department and his country. The State Department initiated an award in his name.

While in Pakistan, Arnie sent a letter home every week that included details of his and Nancy's activities; descriptions of the landscapes, antiquities, and cultural differences they saw; the diplomatic functions they attended and people they met in their travels. He discussed serious matters, yet many of the letters were very funny, especially when travel and events didn't go as planned.

Nancy and I feel there is a book in these letters. Nancy's son John assembled the letters and auxiliary material on a dvd that should make it easier to have a book published.

Every year on August 17th, Nancy brings flowers and prayers to Arnie's grave, accompanied by their best friend Liz Verville, who still serves in the State Department, other associates and family members in the area, and Ruth and me. We dine the night before at Liz's house and have lunch after the services with Nancy.

Nancy

Previous to her marriage to Arnie, Nancy, an attorney at the State Department, was the Assistant Legal Advisor for African Affairs and helped form the basis for the Constitution of Namibia, adopted by their first democratically elected government...among other assignments.

After many months of regaining her strength following Arnie's death, Nancy resumed her work at the State Department. She served as the coordinator for the Balkans where she played a principle role in the Dayton Peace Accords.

Nancy was also the Deputy Assistant Secretary of State for Democracy, Human Rights, and Labor. And she served as

Director of the Office to Monitor and Combat Trafficking in Persons.

Then came Nancy's nomination and confirmation as Ambassador to Slovenia. When she asked Ruth and me, along with Shirley and Milt, to visit her there and stay at the Residence in Ljubljana, our son-in-law Jack had this to say to us. "What! Why are you hesitating? How many U.S. Ambassadors residencies will you be asked to stay?" And so we went and had a great, great visit. Our friends, the Whitmans, accompanied us, billeted at a nearby hotel.

Nancy retired from government work to become the Vice President and Managing Director of Save the Children from which she is currently retired.

Nancy still serves as a member of the Council of Foreign Relations. She divides her time between her country house and gardening in Virginia and the city home in Georgetown she shared with Arnie, filled with mementos of their life together. Nancy enjoys many activities, especially being grandmother to Elizabeth and Katherine, daughters of son Bob Ely and wife Jean; new baby Thalia, daughter of son John Ely and wife Bethany Sanders; and Stephanie's three children with husband Joel Tachau: Aaron, Tova and Sarah.

Extended Family

Billie and Irv Raye and Daughters

Since they live in neighboring Brigantine, it was natural for us to get to know the Rayes as friends rather than just parents of our daughter-in-law Janis.

Very quickly they became part of our family, sharing holidays and birthdays. Billie, who loved Coach bags, even manned the handbag counter for New Year's Day sales at Gordon's Alley.

My best memory of Billie, who is deceased, is at her retirement party. She was sensational, singing and entertaining the crowd of people who were there to honor her service as a teacher and principal.

Irv is our buddy. He comes to dinner twice a week and tries to beat me for answers to questions on the Jeopardy show. I never try to compete with him on geography or sports. He is a whiz. My nephew Steve and Irv have good conversations about the Phillies.

Janis has two sisters: Tammi, who lives in our area, and Lysa in Atlanta. They and Janis are great about visiting their dad. We see Lysa on her frequent visits to Brigantine and keep in touch with Tammi also.

Sylvia, Robbie Gordon, and Their Son Larry

Milton's brother Robbie and wife Sylvia were frequent guests at our house before Robbie died several years ago. Nobody loved our house more than Robbie. He would sit on the second floor porch, look out on the boardwalk, beach, and ocean with such pleasure; it made the rest of us feel good about living here.

And nobody's goodies were more waited for than Sylvia's. She always brought satchels of things to eat. Everybody's favorite was her brownies. They didn't last long and we pestered her to come again or, at least, send more brownies. Sylvia also made us laugh with her half English-half Yiddish witticisms and stories about her mother. Somehow the Yiddish part was the funnier even though I don't understand a word. Sylvia could always put it across.

Norman and Neil, and later Jeffrey, were friends with Slyvia and Robbie's son Larry. On one never forgotten visit, when we and the Gordons were still living in apartments over our store, Larry and Neil had a competition: who could eat the most saltines? I don't remember who won but I do remember the mess and the fun.

Larry became a dentist and married Shelley, an attorney. They hit the jackpot with twins, a boy and a girl: Michael and

Robin. Robin is currently at Columbia University and Michael is at Princeton, a year behind my granddaughter Adrienne.

The Gordon – Raphel Family Home

The two families began their shared life together in three rooms in back of the original Gordon's Youth Shop; then two apartments (over one another) on top of our larger store at Gordon's Alley; and, finally, our "cottage" by the sea—an early 20th century three story shingled house, designed by Stanford White.

This old house has made it possible for the Gordons and Raphels to stay together, to share celebrations with our children and their families, extended family, and friends.

In 2006, for our annual Christmas entertainment, I wrote a short piece to honor the 100th birthday of our house. Our grandchildren Adrienne and Will performed the birthday treatise after a short introduction from me:

THE CENTENNIAL HOUSE
(1906 — 2006)

MURRAY
lt's only a few days until the New Year. And, for our home, it is a very special occasion because it will be 100 years old in 2006. And so we thought this would be a good time to tell our family and friends the history of this very special home. Helping me in this narrative are Will Crowley and Adrienne Raphel who will take the roles of some of the people involved in this centennial celebration.

(beat)
We begin with a little history.

WILL CROWLEY enters.

                    WILL
It all began with a man by the name
of Mahlon Newton. He bought the
property from Jackson to Montgomery
Avenue from the Ocean to Atlantic
Avenue. The property was known as the
"Newton Tract" and sold by Mr. Newton
at the turn of the century to the
Thayer Family from Philadelphia for
$7,800.

ADRIENNE RAPHEL enters.

                    ADRIENNE
The Thayers go back to America's
beginning with a General Thayer
serving under George Washington.
The Thayer hotel in West Point is
named in his honor. The Thayers made
their fortune in the coal country
of Pennsylvania and hired famed
architect Stanford White to design a
summer home in Atlantic City which
they called their "cottage" to use in
the summer.

                    WILL
Stanford White was murdered by Harry
K. Thaw in New York City on June
25, 1906 on the roof of the Saint

Regis Hotel. Thaw accused White of
having an affair with his wife, Evelyn
Nesbitt, a well-known singer and
entertainer. The murder was one of
the most famous crimes of the era.

MURRAY
We wanted to have some way of making
sure Stanford White designed the
house. Mr. Jenkins, the real estate
agent, gave us the name of Mary
Fremont Smith living in Boston who is
the daughter of the Thayers. This is
what she wrote.

ADRIENNE
(reads from piece of paper)
My parents, General and Mrs. Russell
Thayer of Philadelphia, bought the
house. They were so rich and famous
they were invited to sail on the
maiden voyage of an unsinkable ship
called the Titanic where they died
in the boat's sinking. The house,
however, remained in our possession
continuously until my brother died
and the house was sold to a Glenn
Riggs, a radio announcer.

MURRAY
A few years ago I was putting
together a show and was listening to
some old time radio cassettes. This
was the beginning of one of those
tapes: "And now Ladies and Gentlemen,

The Chasse and Sanborn Comedy Hour
wih Edgar Bergen and Charlie McCarthy
and this is your host, Glenn Riggs!"
I said, "WOW — he used to own this
house!" In 1972, Shirley and Ruth
came to me and said...

                    ADRIENNE
"Why can't we have a house instead of
our apartments? Our customers have
houses, why can't we? We work in the
store all day, then come upstairs
and cook dinner, then come down and
straighten up the store for the next
day. We want a house."

                    MURRAY
"A good idea," I said, "with two
conditions: the house must be near
the ocean and it must be in Atlantic
City."

                    ADRIENNE
For two years, we drove up and down
the last streets in Atlantic City
where most of the nice houses were
located. One day, we saw a real
estate agent, Byron Jenkins, putting
a "For Sale" sign in front of this
house.

INSERT — FOR SALE SIGN

                    ADRIENNE (CONT'D)
We always liked this house, stopped

our car and asked him why it was for
sale.

WILL

The owner is selling it because he
doesn't need it anymore.

ADRIENNE

The house was known as the Haunted
House because nobody had lived in it
since 1945. We asked the agent if we
could look inside.

WILL

"Well, I'm nearly 90 years old, and I
can't walk steps too well. And there
are 19 steps up the front. Are you
sure you want me to walk up those
steps?"

ADRIENNE

We looked at one another and thought,
"Maybe he'd get sick or have a
stroke." So we looked at one another
and then said, "OK, we'll buy it!"

WILL

I took the two of them back to my
office and they gave me a check for
$500 as a down payment.

ADRIENNE

We called the store and spoke to
Murray and Milton and said, "We
bought a house!"

MURRAY

I said, "That house needs a lot of work. What's it look like inside?"

ADRIENNE

We hesitated answering and then said, "We didn't look inside."

MURRAY

You didn't look inside? Why not?

ADRIENNE

Well, the real estate agent is 90 years old and there's these 19 steps going up to the front door and we thought, "What if he doesn't make it to the top?" That night the four of us went to look at the house. We were impressed with the layout and design of the house and how much of the original furniture was still there. In the living room we saw magazines from 1945 — *Saturday Evening Post*, *Colliers,* and half-written letters. Nobody had lived in the house for nearly thirty years!

MURRAY

I walked through the house and came back and said to Shirley, "I'd like a return goods label."

WILL

Here's what that meant. In their store if they received a package from a manufacturer and the contents were damaged, they would send it back for credit. But in order to send it back you had to first write the company for a "return goods label" which meant they'd accept the returned package.

ADRIENNE
I asked Murray what was his problem. He said all the bedrooms were on the second and third floors, which was the style at that time. He wanted a bedroom on the first floor. I said we'd build a bedroom on the first floor if that would make him satisfied. He said that was fine.

MURRAY
I called Marty Blumberg who was working on the design and building of the new shops in Gordon's Alley and said, "Please have the electrician and plumber working on the new shops come to this house and put in new plumbing and electricity, but let the rest of the house stay as it was." I also asked Marty to design the new bedroom on the first floor we wanted.

MURRAY
And that's the story of our home.

ADRIENNE
We end with this final note from Mary Dixon Thayer in her letter to us.

```
      (holds up letter)
She wrote, "I am so glad you
appreciate this house and I wish
you great happiness as its present
owner." 2006 is the year our home is
100 years old. And, 100 years ago,
in 1906 is the year that architect
Stanford White died. But he lives
forever in this home.

              MURRAY/ADRIENNE/WILL
Happy birthday to 118 South Newton
Avenue, Atlantic City, New Jersey.
```

Ruth, Shirley, Milton and I give special thanks to Gary Weldon, who, often in consultation with Marty Blumberg, has done all the major changes and repairs to the house for the last 15 years, including the complete remodeling of the first floor kitchen and the sunroom, new floors in the Raphel bedroom and den, and railings where needed for safety. Gary is responsible for keeping our 104-year-old house a home.

We are grateful for good neighbors: the priests from St. Joseph's College who occupy the house directly across from us and welcomed us to the neighborhood; Jodie and Chuck Gowdy at the Atlantic Avenue corner; Sherrie and Bob Weller, our next door neighbors facing the boardwalk; and on our other side, Chipper and John Doherty, who are helpful when we need it and share with us their baker cousin's delicious cakes and cookies.

Photo Gallery

The whole family by the fireplace in Atlantic City

The happy couple on one
of their first dates

Murray with his playwriting buddy,
Jack Lavin, at Syracuse University

The bride and groom

The start of a clothing empire

Ruth and Shirley greet a special guest

Who said nobody would show up for a New Year's Day sale?

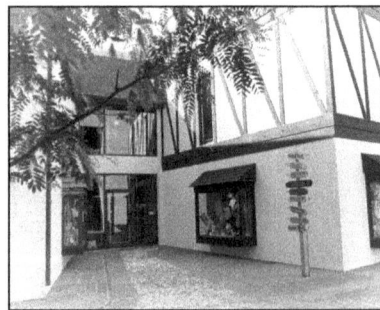

Over 30 shops in Atlantic City

These signs were all over Dublin

Remember . . .

RAPHEL ☑

Freeholder, District No. 2

Murray always loved politics

Receiving an award in Montreux, Switzerland

Ahhhh!!! (Neil and Paula)

Sisters (Paula and Caren)

The kids are growing up

Paula's family

Caren's family

Janis' family

Neil's family

Arnie and Nancy

A family get-together

Four generations

All of Murray and Ruth's grandchildren

Murray's <u>10 Marketing</u> Maxims

"Everybody sells!"

"It is far, far easier to sell more to a customer you have
than to sell to a new customer."

"Your customer asks, 'What's in it for me?'"

"Find out what the customers want...and give it to them."

"The primary sin of advertising is advertising what you want to
sell instead of what your customers want to buy."

"There are only two things people buy:
1. Good feelings
2. Solutions to problems"

"More than 90% of your business comes from repeat customers
or new customers they recommend."

"Change = Danger + Opportunity"

"Cut out the complaints and most people have nothing to say."

"Winners do things now!"

My 3 Favorite Ending Seminar Pieces

• John Paul Getty's Secret of Success: "I got up early, I worked hard, and my father struck oil."

• Question to Sam Walton:
>	"What do you think about the recession?"
>	His answer:
>	"I thought about it, but decided not to participate."

• The Tommy story:

At a busy pre-Christmas time afternoon when I was helping out at the counter, a young man named Tommy asked if he could use the telephone.

"Sure, Tommy," I said. I knew Tommy all his life. I delivered his baby clothes to his mother at the hospital when he was born.

He picked up the phone and dialed a number. I heard him say, "Hi. I just went past your house and saw you had a big lawn. I cut lawns for extra money. I also trim hedges. And I was wondering if..."

He paused, listened and then continued, "I see. Are you satisfied with the work?"

Another pause.

"Well, would it be all right if I called you back in a month or so to see if you're still satisfied? I can. Thank you." And he hung up.

I walked over to him and said, "Tommy, forgive me. But I was standing here and heard your conversation. I want you to know that everything you said was right. Promise you won't be disappointed because you didn't get the sale."

"Oh, Mr. Raphel," he said, "I have the sale. That was one of my customers. I was just checking up to see how I'm doing."

Murray Raphel Serves

Murray Serves as:

Vice President, Historic Gardner's Basin

He Served as:

*Member, National Advisory Council of the Small Business
    Administration (SBA)*

Vice Chairman, NJ Casino Reinvestment Development Authority

State Commissioner, Atlantic City Convention Center Authority

Director, Board of Freeholders, Atlantic County, New Jersey

Chairman, Atlantic County Improvement Authority

Board Chairman, Atlantic Community College

Chairman, Atlantic City Parking Authority

Vice President, Miss America Pageant

His Awards:

Montreux International Award for Excellence in Direct Marketing

Atlantic City Hall of Fame, inducted as Charter Member 1993

New Jersey Retailer of the Year

Albert Galatin Award as one of America's outstanding businesses

Books by Murray Raphel

By Murray

How to Promote an Infants' & Children's Wear Store

But Would Saks Fifth Avenue Do It?

Mind Your Own Business

Mind Your Own Business...Supermarket Edition

Customerization

Selling Rules!

Speaking Rules!

By Murray and Ray Considine

The Great Brain Robbery

By Murray and Ken Erdman

The Do-It-Yourself Direct Marketing Handbook

By Murray and Neil Raphel

Tough Selling for Tough Times

Up the Loyalty Ladder

By Murray and Neil Raphel and Janis Raye

The Complete Idiot's Guide to Winning Customer Loyalty

Client List of Murray Raphel

Food Associations

AECOC, Spain
Canadian Council
Grocery Distributors
Food Distributors
International
Food Marketing Institute (FMI)
Frozen Food Association
IGA, headquarters
and retailers
Irish Food & Fisheries Board
National Grocers Association
(NGA)
Private Label Expo
State Associations: keynote
speaker for 25 State
conventions and
Canada

Food Retailers

Autry Greer & Sons
Genuardi Super Markets Inc.
Giant Food Stores, PA
Hy-Vee, Inc.
Jewel Supermarkets
Jitney Jungle
King Soopers
Price Chopper, NY
Market Basket Food Stores
Winn-Dixie Stores

Food Wholesaling/ Distributing

Agora Food Merchants, Canada
Associated Wholesale Grocers, KS
Associated Wholesalers of PA
Atlantic Wholesalers, Canada
Certified Angus Beef
Copps Foods
Fleming Foods
Grocers Supply
Kesko, Finland
Millbrook Distribution Services
Piggly Wiggly Carolina Co.
Sobey's Inc., Canada
Spartan Stores, Inc.
Supervalu
United Grocers

Manufacturers

Crowley Foods
J & J Snack Foods
Scania Trucks, Sweden
Smith,Kline &Beecham,
Australia&NewZea.

Communications

Cable Advertising Bureau
Cornerstone Media
Cox Communications
Lebensmittel Zeitung, Germany
Newspaper Advertising
Association

Promo Magazine
WEKA Publishing, German

Direct Marketing
An Post (Irish Post Office)
Atelier America, Canada
CapStar
Direct Marketing to Business
    (DMB)
Epsilon
IMS Internationl
    (Div. Of Dun & Brad)
New York Direct Marketing Day
Nordic, German, Finnish,
    Irish & Spanish Direct
    Marketing Associations
Presidential Card, Australia
Project Planning,
    Northern Ireland
Retail Business Solutions, Sweden
Scribendi AB, Sweden
Symposiums: Montreux,
    Switzerland; Pan
    Pacific, Sydney,
    Australia
Walter Schmid, Switzerland
ZFU, Switzerland
Seminars world wide

Financial Marketing
AMP, Australia
Credit Suisse, Switzerland
Customer Insight
Heinrich Marketing
International Banking
    Technologies

Irish Life Insurance Company
Life Underwriters Association,
    Toronto
Million Dollar Roundtable
National Commerce
    Bank Services
National Westminister Bank, NJ
Top of the Table

Retailing
American Express,
    US, United Kingdom
ArtExpo
Blarney Woolen Mills, Ireland
Broyhill Furniture
Factory Outlet Stores
Greenwich Workshop
International Mass Retailers
    Association
Kall Kwik, UK
Kwik Kopy
National Home Furnishings
    Association
National Sporting Goods
    Association
NCR Corporation
Professional Audio Video
    Retailers Association
Retail Business Solutions,
    Sweden
Spector Photo Finishing,
    Belgium
STS Systems
Trump Castle Hotel & Casino